THE WORLD COUNCIL
OF CHURCHES & POLITICS

Freedom House

Freedom House is an independent nonprofit organization that monitors human rights and political freedom around the world. Established in 1941, Freedom House believes that effective advocacy of civil rights at home and human rights abroad must be grounded in fundamental democratic values and principles.

In international affairs, Freedom House continues to focus attention on human rights violations by oppressive regimes, both of the left and the right. At home, we stress the need to guarantee all citizens not only equal rights under law, but equal opportunity for social and economic advancement.

Freedom House programs and activities include bimonthly and annual publications, conferences and lecture series, public advocacy, ongoing research of political and civil liberties around the globe, and selected, on-site monitoring to encourage fair elections.

Focus on Issues

General Editor: James Finn

This publication is one in a series of Focus on Issues. The separate publications in this series differ in the method of examination and breadth of the study, but each focuses on a single, significant political issue of our time. The series represents one aspect of the extensive program of Freedom House. The views expressed are those of the authors and not necessarily those of the Board of Freedom House.

About the Author

J.A. Emerson Vermaat has been reporting in the Dutch press on meetings and Assemblies of the World Council of Churches since 1973. He writes and lectures on WCC activities with a wide and intimate knowledge of its past history and present operations.

A graduate in law of Leiden University, the Netherlands, Mr. Vermaat has specialized in East-West relations, Latin America and human rights issues. His articles have appeared in a large number of leading newspapers and journals both in Europe and America. He is presently editor of a current affairs program on Dutch TV.

THE WORLD COUNCIL OF CHURCHES & POLITICS
1975-1986

J.A. Emerson Vermaat

Focus on Issues No. 6

FREEDOM HOUSE

First published 1989.

Cover design by Emerson Wajdowicz Studios, N.Y.C.

Library of Congress Cataloging-in-Publication Data
Vermaat, J.A.E.
The World Council of Churches & Politics, 1975-1986

Focus on Issues : no. 6
Includes index.
1. World Council of Churches—Controversial literature. 2. Christianity and politics. I. Title. II.Title: World Council of Churches and politics.
III. Series: Focus on Issues (Freedom House (U.S.)) ; no. 6.
BX6.W78V4   1989   270.8'2'0601   88-30956
ISBN 0-932088-30-9
ISBN 0-932088-29-5 (pbk.)

Distributed by arrangement with:

UPA, Inc.
4720 Boston Way
Lanham, MD 20706

3 Henrietta Street
London, WC2E 8LU England

Contents

Introduction   1

The Soviet Bloc: 9
A "Selective Silence"

Monitoring Human Rights in Asia   27

"Threats to Peace":   39
Conflict and Compromise

Central American Liberation Theology   51

Southern Africa and the WCC's   65
"Program to Combat Racism"

At Odds in the Middle East   77

Nuclear Disarmament: 85
Tilting Toward the Soviet Line

New Directions for the WCC   95

Notes   105

Index   123

Introduction

"We have to make our insights and our wisdom happen, and for that you cannot escape institutions."[1]
—Dr. Philip Potter, general secretary
World Council of Churches, 1973-1984

Churches today sometimes resemble political institutions more than religious ones. In particular, major ecumenical organizations like the National Council of Churches (NCC), and the Geneva-based World Council of Churches (WCC) are becoming increasingly politicized. To be sure, they do have a long tradition of political pronouncements, but never have their statements been so controversial and so much under attack as they are today. Many people in the pew as well as many outsiders feel that current "church politics" testify to biased political attitudes of a church élite that has stopped taking its critics seriously.

With its more than 300 member churches, the WCC supposedly speaks for non-Catholic Christendom. Many in the WCC's member churches, however, are critical of or indifferent to it and if afforded the chance to hear what is pronounced in their name they would, no doubt, raise their voices in strong protest. Many have already done so. Others left churches in which they no longer felt at home. They need the church for their spiritual needs and not for the drawing up of political programs. Thus, polarization, dwindling memberships and other signs of dilapidation are the trend in most major WCC oriented churches in the West, while religious movements outside the WCC's aegis are blossoming.

Origins of the WCC
The WCC grew out of the so-called "ecumenical movement" which, from its inception, was marked by diversity. It was made up of various ecclesiastical traditions, theological trends and schools. Having its roots primarily in a major missionary movement in the nineteenth century, the ecumenical

movement as such began to take shape at the World Missionary Conference at Edinburgh in 1910. "Cooperation and unity" had been a recurrent theme at nineteenth-century missionary conferences. It was correctly felt that without a united front at home missionary endeavors in the field were bound to be less effective. This resulted in the creation of the "International Missionary Council" (IMC) in 1921.[2]

Other roots of the emerging ecumenical movement were the nineteenth-century student and revival movements which sprang up as a result of the preaching of such men as Dwight L. Moody, Charles H. Spurgeon and Charles Finney. They inspired thousands of students to go to the mission field. Today one would call such movements "fundamentalist" or "evangelical." Other influences, however, played their part as well. A movement much more concerned about social ethics and politics than theological issues or "doctrine" was the "Social Gospel" movement. Having its origins in nineteenth-century liberal theology, the "Social Gospel" was essentially an idealistic, optimist and activist movement. It cherished the idea of a world being gradually transformed into the Kingdom of God by human endeavor. It called for a "practical Christianity" and was among the factors producing the so-called "Life and Work" movement which, in 1925, held its first major "World Conference" in Stockholm.

Movements stressing ecclesiastical unity and theological doctrine united under the banner of "Faith and Order" which first convened at Lausanne in 1927. Although there was much overlap and interchange, the missionary and student movements continued to exist independently of these two major bodies which formed the WCC in 1948. Plans for the creation of a "World Council of Churches" had already been made in the second part of the 1930s.

Fearing that the future WCC might be dominated by the more politically oriented "Life and Work," the International Missionary Council decided not to join it. Criticism was also heard in "Faith and Order." The main spokesman for the critics was the Anglican Bishop of Gloucester, Dr. A.C. Headlam, who told the "Second World Conference on Faith and Order" in Edinburgh, 1937:

> I am sorry, but I wish to record my opposition to the proposal for the creation of a World Council of Churches. I do not know how many there are who are opposed to it, but there is a definite body of members opposed to any definite connection with the Life and Work movement.

2

If such a Council were to exist, and if it passed resolutions on public affairs, it might do a very considerable amount of harm. Resolutions passed by churches in the past on political matters, etc., have often appeared hasty and not sufficiently thought out, and are as likely to do harm as good.[3]

Headlam's prophetic warning was ignored and Faith and Order joined the WCC. Unlike Life and Work, however, Faith and Order preserved its name. Today Faith and Order issues still take a prominent place within the WCC. But the final goal of doctrinal consensus or ecclesiastical unity seems to have been superseded by political issues causing new controversy and dissension.

Eventually the IMC joined the WCC in 1961. Before the Second World War the ecumenical movement was largely an affair of Western churches. This began to change after 1961. Churches and theologians from Africa, Asia and Latin America increasingly began to influence the ecumenical debate and profoundly affected the WCC's outlook on society and politics. In the 1970s "liberation theology," whose origins lie in Latin America, with its Marxist leanings, made deep inroads in the WCC. Consequently, it negatively affected relations between the WCC and the Vatican which had repeatedly denounced "liberation theology."

An outline of the WCC's organization

The WCC is a complex organization. At its heart is the General Secretariat led by the general secretary. Although the WCC general secretary can make statements, he can only speak on behalf of the Council when empowered to do so by a more representative body. The most representative body of the WCC is its Assembly, which meets every seven or eight years. (Between 1948 and 1983 there were six such Assemblies.) Between subsequent Assemblies, the WCC's Central Committee meets annually to review the work done by the WCC and its staff, to approve the budget, and to launch and stimulate new programs. Its statements reflect the official policy of the WCC since all its member churches are represented in the Central Committee. The Central Committee's 150 members are elected by the Assembly. Statements made by the "Executive Committee"— a much smaller inner body consisting of nineteen members (sixteen of which are elected by the Central Committee, the other three are the moderator and two vice-moderators)—are less representative of the WCC but certainly have authoritative status. The Executive Committee acts on behalf of the Central Committee between its meetings (i.e., the meetings of the Central Committee).

Usually the Central Committee confirms the decisions taken by the Executive Committee. Finally, there are the "officers" of the WCC (moderator, vice-moderators of the Central Committee as well as the general secretary) the general secretary himself and various "spokespersons" of the WCC. They, too, can issue statements but their authority is usually limited unless subsequently endorsed by a more representative body.

The WCC has seven presidents that are elected by the Assembly. The WCC's vast program area is divided into three major "Program Units" that in turn are subdivided as follows:

Program Unit 1: Faith and Witness
  • Faith and Order
  • World Mission and Evangelism
  • Church and Society
  • Dialogue with People of Living Faiths and Ideologies

Program Unit 2: Justice and Service
  • Churches' Participation in Development
  • International Affairs
  • Program to Combat Racism
  • Interchurch Aid, Refugee and World Service
  • Christian Medical Commission

Program Unit 3: Education and Renewal
  • Education
  • Women in Church and Society
  • Renewal and Congregational Life
  • Youth
  • Theological Education

The work of each of the three program units is supervised, reviewed and coordinated by a "Unit Committee" which annually issues a report to the Central Committee. Although the other program units cannot be ignored, much emphasis is presently given to Program Unit 2 (Justice and Service). Every year, the Central Committee adopts a number of so-called "public issues." These are Unit 2-related statements on the political situation in a given country or on trends in international affairs. Because some of these statements are rather controversial, the WCC has gained a reputation for being pro-leftist and anti-Western. Consequently, its many other activities in the field of, for example, humanitarian aid or faith and doctrine, draw less and less attention and are hardly ever picked up by the international media.

One of the WCC's activities which attracts much attention is its "Program to Combat Racism" (PCR), established by the Central Committee in 1969 as a typical action-oriented program.

> The program draws attention to policies of governments and transnational corporations which give economic support to racism, examines how theology is used to promote racism and how it might also combat it. [4]

There is also the PCR's "Special Fund" which financially supports organizations of the racially oppressed. Since its inception, the bulk of grants from the "Special Fund" went to "liberation movements" in Southern Africa. Other recipients include, for example, Australian aboriginals and Indian groups in North and Latin America.

The WCC's Commission on International Affairs

An important event in the history of the WCC was the creation of a "Commission of the Churches of International Affairs" (CCIA) by the Provisional Committee of the WCC and the International Missionary Council in 1946. The WCC's activities in the field of international affairs were then institutionalized and coordinated. The CCIA was set up as a consulting body on the broad spectrum of international affairs, with special emphasis on human rights, racism, religious freedom and international organization. Having the status of Non-Governmental Organization (NGO) with the United Nations, the CCIA has kept in close touch with the United Nations and other international bodies. CCIA staff members officially attend all U.N. General Assemblies and major U.N. conferences. Due to the diplomatic skill of its first director, Dr. O. Frederick Nolde, a Lutheran from the United States, the CCIA played a significant role in the formation of several important international documents on human rights.[5]

At the time of the Uppsala Assembly in 1968, it was felt that the CCIA had been dominated by staff members from Western countries for too long a time. Important changes, it was deemed, should take place. In 1969 Dr. Leopoldo Niilus, a lawyer and an Argentine national of Latvian origin, was, with Russian Orthodox support, appointed as new CCIA director.[6]

Support for Dr. Niilus could be explained by his previous involvement in the Prague-based Christian Peace Conference (CPC), listed by the U.S. Department of State as a front organization of the International Department of the Central Committee of the Communist Party of the Soviet Union (ID-CPSU).[7]

Dr. Niilus had also been involved in another leftist organization, "Church and Society in Latin America" (ISAL), as well as the "World Student Christian Federation" (WSCF). The latter organization takes extreme leftist views on East-West relations, the PLO and support to armed guerrillas. Under Niilus the CCIA soon adopted political lines considered favorably by the Soviets who tightened their grip on the CCIA. Particularly after the WCC's Nairobi Assembly in 1975 the CCIA began to concern itself much more with peace and disarmament issues.

Since 1982 the CCIA has been led by Ninan R. Koshy from India. Like Niilus, Koshy had previously been active in the CPC (as a member of its International Secretariat) and the WSCF.

The role of Soviet fronts

Although the WCC is not a Soviet front organization, Soviet Communist party fronts, particularly the CPC, do exert some influence on it. Subsequent CCIA Directors Niilus and Koshy attended major events of the Soviet-controlled World Peace Council (WPC) in Sofia in 1980 and Prague in 1983. The present general secretary of the WCC, Dr. Emilio Castro (from Uruguay), has also been involved in the Christian Peace Conference for some time. In April and May 1964 he took a long trip to Eastern Europe, forty days of which were spent in the Soviet Union and ten days in Prague. In Prague he attended the "Second World Congress of Christians for Peace," sponsored by the CPC.[8] Another Third World theologian who had been close to the WCC and the CPC, Julio de Santa Ana, was very influential in promoting "liberation theology" within the WCC. De Santa Ana was a member of the International Secretariat of the CPC from 1964 to 1970. The WCC published several of De Santa Ana's books; he was with the WCC's department for development.

Furthermore, two successive WCC presidents, Metropolitan Nikodim of Leningrad, and Metropolitan Gregorios of New Delhi, played leading roles in the CPC. Gregorios is still very active in it. Involvement by WCC officials and dignitaries in known Soviet front organizations was opposed by the first general secretary of the WCC, Dr. W.A. Visser 't Hooft. His successors, however, have taken a different line. In particular, Dr. Philip Potter did not hesitate to cooperate occasionally with the Helsinki-based World Peace Council (WPC) led by the Indian Communist Romesh Chandra. For example, Potter and Chandra were among the "officers" of a "Disarmament Conference" convened by the Special NGO committee on Disarmament in Geneva in 1982 and organized by the CCIA's executive secretary, Mr. Victor W.C. Hsu. Other Soviet Communist party fronts participating in the event were the Afro-Asian People's Solidarity Organization (AAPSO), the Women's International Democratic Federation (WIDF) and the World Federation of Democratic Youth (WFDY).[9]

Romesh Chandra, a staunch defender of the Soviet invasion of Afghanistan, also attended a WCC sponsored "informal exchange of views" on the prevention of nuclear war chaired by CCIA Director Ninan Koshy in March 1984. A few months later, the CCIA and the WPC were among the main sponsors behind an "International Conference on Nicaragua and for Peace in Central America" held in Lisbon. Portuguese Prime Minister Mario Soares successfully prevented his friends in the Socialist International from sending important delegates to this meeting. In a letter to Social-Democratic sister parties Soares indicated that the Lisbon meeting basically was a Communist inspired event.[10]

All these examples show that during the period of 1975-86 the WCC did not distance itself too much from known Soviet front groups. It should be further noted that both the fronts and the WCC often simultaneously developed their major themes, particularly in the field of peace and disarmament and some Third World issues. But most influence on the WCC was not exerted directly by the fronts themselves but by individuals with some kind of background in one of those fronts.

This was one of the reasons why many of the WCC's statements on international affairs so markedly coincided with Soviet views and positions, particularly in the period under review (1975-86). In addition, the Russian Orthodox church often played a decisive role in preventing the WCC from making statements which strongly deviated from the Soviet line. Consequently, such statements were not altogether absent, but they were few. Under Mikhail Gorbachev, the Soviets tend to shift emphasis from the traditional fronts to organizations more acceptable to Western audiences. Neverthless, the fronts continue to play a role in Soviet Communist propaganda.

The Soviet Bloc:
A "Selective Silence"

The Yakunin-Regelson letter

Two days after the 1975 World Council of Churches Assembly opened
in Nairobi, the Assembly's daily newspaper, *Target,* published an "Appeal
for WCC Action on Behalf of Persecuted Christians." The appeal was signed
by two members of the Russian Orthodox church—Gleb Yakunin, a priest,
and Lev Regelson, a layman.[1] It immediately drew a sympathetic response
from many delegates.

Within the World Council of Churches, wrote Yakunin and Regelson,
"the matter of religious persecution (has) failed to take its due place—
although it ought to become the central theme of Christian ecumenism."
The WCC, the Russians charged, was silent "when the Russian Orthodox
Church was half destroyed" by Soviet persecution in the 1960s. "No indig-
nant protest was heard...even when religion was completely crushed in
Albania—and the WCC still remained silent even after a priest had been
shot to death in Albania for having baptized a baby."[2]

The points raised by the courageous Russians' letter are vital in exam-
ining the manner in which the WCC has addressed international issues
during the past decade. Though the Council has always deemed the protection of human rights among its major obligations, the organization has
repeatedly declined to publicly protest religious repression and human
rights violations in Eastern Europe. The WCC has maintained this policy
even though some member churches—especially those from the Netherlands and Switzerland—have occasionally protested. On several occasions,
WCC officials have attempted to defend the Council's policy toward Eastern bloc governments. In 1972, for example, WCC General Secretary Eu-

gene Carson Blake, replying to an expression of concern by the General Synod of Reformed Churches in the Netherlands, defended the policy by arguing that protests by Western churches, or by the WCC, might harm Eastern European churches that belong to the Council:

> I know that a policy in which the difference of situations is disregarded may help the public image of the World Council of Churches, but I am not willing to pay such a price for our image. More important than the image of the World Council is the quality of our fellowship, and a genuine fellowship expresses itself through differentiated approaches according to the real needs of those suffering discrimination.[3]

In the same statement, Blake acknowledged that there is evidence of religious persecution in Eastern Europe:

> Although a hostile Western press may often exaggerate the number of really persecuted Christians and the fate befalling them, there are too many open letters sent by Protestant and Orthodox Christians alike, too many people who are sent to labor camps or kept in psychiatric institutions, too many churches and monasteries closed, to believe that there are not regular actions carried out against minorities which live from sources other than the prevailing ideology...
>
> The World Council of Churches is not unaware of this situation and knows that many of its general pronouncements on human rights are as much applicable in Eastern Europe as in Southeast Asia, North America, southern Africa, and Latin America.

Nonetheless, Blake questioned the prudence of public responses to reports of religious repression in Eastern Europe:

> Several of our leaders and staff members have made démarches to government officials in socialist countries in order to advocate greater freedom for the churches...We have often found that such approaches are more successful than public declarations.[4]

Blake argued that reliable information about events in Eastern Europe is difficult to obtain, and must be gained from research centers which specialize in Eastern European affairs. Second, he said that Western and Third World churches need to get to know Eastern European churches better than is presently the case. "Our expression of critical concern becomes cheap and can only be understood in the countries concerned as anti-Communist, i.e., political declarations," Blake suggested. He recommended programs of regular communication, visitation and exchange.

The same perspective was defended in 1974 at a WCC-sponsored conference in Austria on "Human Rights and Christian Responsibility." There, WCC staff members argued that Eastern European Christians would be placed in a difficult position if the WCC were to publicly protest human rights abuses by their governments.

This policy of what might be termed "selective silence" about reported religious repression in Eastern Europe has characterized WCC pronouncements for many years. It was repeated several times; in 1981, Ninan Koshy, director of the Council's Commission of the Churches on International Affairs (CCIA), said in an interview:

> We should not indulge in an ecclesiastical running commentary on world affairs. We have to make a selection and make no apology for it. It is basically the situation of the churches in each country that determines whether our public statement will be effective.[5]

It is the general policy of the WCC that any WCC action on reports of human rights abuses must be preceded by consultation with representatives of WCC member churches in the countries involved. WCC leaders prefer to involve the Russian Orthodox church, or the Union of Evangelical Christian Baptists, when reviewing reports of religious persecution in the Soviet Union. The difficulties of such an approach are evident. It severely reduces the likelihood of a WCC protest about conditions in Eastern Europe. In fact, state-controlled churches of the Eastern bloc virtually enjoy veto power over WCC pronouncements related to that region of the world.

The WCC leadership believes, in essence, that "quiet diplomacy" is more effective than public pronouncements or protests with Communist governments. For this reason, the WCC does not openly criticize the policies of North Korea, the People's Republic of China or Cuba, while repeatedly commenting on the policies of, say, South Africa, the Republic of China (Taiwan) or the United States.

There is more than strategy involved in the WCC policy, however, for the Council has for years revealed a bias in favor of revolutionary socialist movements and governments. There is every reason to believe that key

WCC staff members sympathize with revolutionists in Nicaragua, Cuba, Vietnam—before the collapse of South Vietnam in 1975 their sympathy was with North Vietnam—and the Communist People's Republic of China. More than once these governments have been given favorable treatment in the ecumenical press, expressed in the language of "solidarity with the poor and oppressed," "human rights," and "the Gospel." The "poor and oppressed" of Eastern Europe, however, are seldom mentioned in these WCC communications. Explaining this dichotomy, a WCC spokesman said:

> To be sure, the Council has never claimed neutrality; after all, the Gospel which it seeks to express is biased in favor of those who have least and suffer most. When you survey the WCC's one hundred plus public statements in the seven years since the Nairobi Assembly (1975), you can see that there has clearly been no attempt to even up issues and areas. Statements on human rights and repression outnumber those on doctrinal theology and unity. Appeals for emergency relief outnumber calls for interfaith dialogue. Africa is addressed more often than Eastern Europe.[6]

The human rights debate at Nairobi
Given these sentiments and sympathies, many WCC leaders and staff members at the Nairobi Assembly were annoyed by the Yakunin-Regelson letter. Its bluntness contrasted with the carefully modulated tone that the WCC maintains in addressing human rights issues in Eastern Europe. In the wake of the controversy that followed the letter, the Nairobi Assembly was in many respects an exercise in damage control for the WCC leadership, which was determined to limit the debate instigated by the dissidents.

As things turned out, the official response at Nairobi to the Yakunin-Regelson letter was rather poor. Nor has there been any forthright WCC response to reports of religious repression in Eastern Europe, and especially the Soviet Union, in the decade since the Nairobi Assembly. Instead, the Council's predisposition to revolutionary ideology, and its insistence on "silent diplomacy," have enabled the Soviet Union to escape profound criticism about its human rights policies.

Another important example of the WCC's selective commentary on international issues arose at Nairobi in a debate over a draft report entitled "Angola: Independence and Intervention." As proposed, the report condemned the government of South Africa for its involvement in Angolan affairs, but proposals to identify the role of other powers (Cuba, Soviet Union) failed to be incorporated in the final text.

A similar debate arose during the Assembly over a proposed statement on "Human Rights in Latin America." WCC General Secretary Philip Potter dismissed a Belgian pastor's proposal that the same type of statement be drafted to address "Human Rights in the Soviet Union." Potter ruled that the subject under Assembly review was Latin America, not the Soviet Union.[7]

Assembly delegates, many of whom sympathized with the Yakunin-Regelson letter, were naturally frustrated by these developments. A group of them brought up Eastern Europe when the Assembly turned to a general statement on the ten principles of the recently signed Helsinki Accords on European Security and Cooperation, which, *inter alia*, provided for the protection of human rights. This was a strategic move because the Soviet Union was a chief signatory to the Helsinki Accords; there were enough reports of repre.sion in the Soviet Union to warrant WCC attention.

Swiss delegate Jacques Rossel was applauded by many delegates when he proposed that the Assembly amend its statement on "Disarmament, the Helsinki Agreement and Religious Liberty" to include the following text:

The WCC is concerned about restrictions of religious freedom particularly in the USSR. The Assembly respectfully requests the government of the USSR to implement effectively principle No. 7 ("Respect for human rights and fundamental freedoms, including the freedom of thought, conscience, religion, or belief") of the Helsinki Agreement.[8]

The amendment was immediately seconded by Richard Holloway of the Episcopal church in Scotland.

In the debate that ensued, Rossel's proposal was considerably muted. The first opposition came, not surprisingly, from the Russian Orthodox church delegation. Metropolitan Yuvenaliy objected that Rossel's proposal offended Christian fellowship. Metropolitan Nikodim said human rights in the Soviet Union had not been sufficiently studied to allow such a condemnation of Soviet policy.

These objections succeeded in changing the tone of the debate, which briefly adjourned following confusion over a point of order. When the discussion of Rossel's proposal resumed, a substitute amendment was recommended by Canadian Anglican Archbishop Edward W. Scott:

The WCC is concerned about the restriction to religious liberty in many parts of the world, including the USSR. It is grateful for the leadership the government of the USSR gave in the development of the Helsinki Agreement and calls upon it and all governments to give full implementation to Section 7 of that Agreement.[9]

Scott's proposal was referred to a drafting committee, consisting of Tahi B. Simatupang of Indonesia, William B. Thompson of the United Presbyterian church, U.S.A., and Alexey Buevski of the Russian Orthodox church. The drafters proposed a compromise text:

> The Assembly recognizes that churches in different parts of Europe are living and working under very different conditions and traditions. Political systems, constitutions, and administrative practice vary from nation to nation. In most Western European countries the churches have the opportunity to seek to reach people through many different public media and to organize special groups for young people and others. In the absence of such possibilities in many eastern countries, the churches reach people, including youth, through religious education of children in the family, catechizing in the church of interested persons, and vital public worship.[10]

Buevski said the compromise was conceived "in the spirit of brotherly love, mutual understanding, and the spirit of fellowship, overcoming division."[11] The Assembly accepted the compromise and so a veil was drawn over the plight of the religiously persecuted in the Soviet Union.

The Yakunin-Regelson letter also threatened the expected election at Nairobi of Metropolitan Nikodim, leader of the Russian Orthodox delegation, to one of the WCC's seven presidential positions. The problem lay not within the Eastern bloc countries: the thirty-member delegation from the Russian Orthodox church, the largest at Nairobi, had been thoroughly instructed by the official Soviet Council for Religious Affairs, and most of the additional eighty delegates from Eastern bloc churches were under Nikodim's control as well. The problem lay with Third World delegates. Their support, which Nikodim needed for election, was thought to be shaky as a result of the revelations about Soviet religious repression.

The Russians immediately responded to this difficulty. On 5 December 1975, with the WCC Assembly well underway, delegates from mainly Third World churches were invited to a meeting with the Christian Peace Conference (CPC), a Prague-based front for the Soviet Communist Party whose leader was none other than Metropolitan Nikodim.[12] At the meeting, the Third World delegates were reminded of the Moscow Patriarchate's influence with the Soviet government, and warned of the consequences to their own governments and countries if the delegates did not support Nikodim's nomination to a WCC presidency. Among the inducements mentioned were Soviet and Eastern European aid to Third World countries and other Soviet-sponsored assistance to liberation movements.[13] Nikodim was subsequently elected to a WCC presidency with much Third World support.

In spite of their apparent successes, the Russian Orthodox delegates were not entirely satisfied with the Nairobi Assembly. The Russians would have protested even the compromise agreement to the statement on "Disarmament, the Helsinki Agreement and Religious Liberty" had not one of their own delegates, Buevski, an executive secretary of the Moscow Patriarchate's foreign relations department, been one of its drafters. The Russians were also unhappy with the amendment successfully proposed by Rossel and Holloway when those two delegates realized that their original recommendation would not prevail. Their substitute stated:

The Assembly requests the General Secretary to see that the question of religious liberty be the subject of intensive consultations with the member churches of the signatory states of the Helsinki Agreement and that a first report be presented at the next Central Committee meeting in August 1976.

When this amended text was finally accepted, the Russians decided to abstain from voting on the document as a whole. They argued that they "were disappointed by the prevailing atmosphere which surrounded the discussion of these questions at the Assembly, an atmosphere compounded of haste, nerves and divisiveness."[14] Nonetheless, the Assembly adopted the revised Rossel-Holloway amendment.

The Russian Orthodox church's protests continued after the close of the Assembly. Patriarch Pimen of the Russian church immediately wrote to Potter and Dr. Edward W. Scott, who was moderator of the WCC's Central Committee, to decry "the haste with which the so-called silence of the Assembly regarding our country was broken, and by the resultant unfriendly spirit which arose." Pimen also complained that representatives of churches from socialist countries had been prevented from presenting their views. He chided the Council for dealing "directly with (ecclesiastical dissidents) bypassing church leadership, which we regard as an act of overt or covert distrust of our church authority or an attempt to sow distrust." Further actions of this kind could, Pimen warned, "lead to a weakening of our ties with the WCC."[15]

In Moscow, the Soviet government's Council for Religious Affairs organized a campaign among clergy and lay church members to protest the WCC statement and to neutralize the Yakunin-Regelson letter.[16] A similar campaign was planned in Budapest where Eastern bloc church representatives met to discuss a common strategy for addressing the human rights issue.

The object of these campaigns was clear: to tell the World Council of Churches that WCC criticism of Soviet-bloc governments would come at a heavy cost—perhaps even a breakup of the international ecumenical movement. The longer-term objective was equally clear: the Soviets were determined to mute criticism of their human rights record by gaining greater influence within the WCC's highest echelons.

The Soviets' strategy has had mixed success. The WCC's 1976 colloquium on the Helsinki Act held in Montreux, Switzerland, for example, reiterated the importance of addressing human rights: "Condemnation of violations of human rights wherever they are objectively established is an obligation of the churches and should not be confused with unjustified interference."[17]

But the Montreux colloquium made the intentions of Eastern bloc churches and governments appear benign. Delegates at Montreux were quick to acknowledge the importance of "Christian-Marxist dialogue," and, with a nod to the West, condemned "Cold War attitudes still alive (which) contradict the spirit of Helsinki." Furthermore, the Montreux meeting commended a June 1976 statement by European Communist leaders meeting in East Berlin that had affirmed the importance of governmental cooperation with religious communities and believers, and pledged dialogue with them.[18]

The East Berlin meeting took place on the eve of a major Soviet-orchestrated peace campaign throughout Europe. The campaign served many purposes, one of which was to divert public attention from human rights issues in Communist states. Shortly afterwards, the Montreux colloquium ended with a recommendation that churches from socialist countries be given opportunity to make greater contributions to all levels of WCC programs.[19]

In August of 1976, the WCC's Central Committee repeated that Eastern European churches should have increased participation in the Council. In addition, the WCC began to suggest the interrelation between human rights and other international issues. For example, General Secretary Philip Potter said in his report on the Montreux Colloquium to the Central Committee that the struggle for human rights and religious freedom around the world could be pursued only when "other realities" were addressed. These realities, he said, included such issues as disarmament, coexistence between the superpowers, détente and international cooperation. There was, Potter explained, a "dialectical relationship" among issues that the WCC could not ignore.[20] The same view had repeatedly been propounded at international conferences by delegates from Eastern European churches.

Potter recommended that the August 1976 meeting authorize the creation of two bodies. One would operate within the Commission of the Churches on International Affairs (CCIA) "as a stimulus and as a means of sharing ideas and experiences among churches."[21] This would be the "Human Rights Advisory Group." The other would exist apart from the CCIA and be composed of representatives of churches from countries which had signed the Helsinki Accords. From the latter would evolve "The Churches' Human Rights Program for the Implementation of the Helsinki Final Act."

Potter's proposal seemed like a good one. In fact, it satisfied many of the delegates who had been most outspoken on the issue at the Nairobi Assembly. As later events proved, however, the proposal did little to clear the air of disappointment and disagreement. As Bishop Per Loenning of Norway remarked:

When the devil wants nothing to happen he first sets up a committee! Our Central Committee must clearly voice the spirit of Nairobi... It is right to stress the interrelatedness of religious freedom and human rights as a whole, but we must not run the risk that the real issues we face disappear in foggy contextuality. On issues of racism, peace, and war the WCC has not spoken so circumspectly as to allow these issues to disappear. Neither should we do so with religious freedom.[22]

Eastern bloc churches expressed official opposition to Potter's proposal for formation of a "Churches' Human Rights Program for the Implementation of the Helsinki Final Act." They need not have worried. Essentially nothing transpired and, two years later, in January of 1979, the Central Committee reported in its review of the Human Rights Advisory Group that, due to lack of funds, the CCIA had not even convened the group members.[23]

17

Strengthening ties to Eastern Europe

As the years passed, the relationship deepened between the WCC and its member churches from Eastern Europe. Churches from Hungary took the lead, as in the past, in endorsing decidedly pro-Soviet policies. For example, in March of 1977, the Hungarian Ecumenical Council hosted a meeting of WCC officials and representatives from Eastern European churches. A year later, the president of the Hungarian State Office for Religious Affairs visited WCC headquarters in Geneva and praised the "positive role" the ecumenical movement was playing in promoting European security and cooperation:

> We set great value on the fact that it successfully resists the Cold War attempts, whereby new possibilities open up before the WCC to work even more effectively for international peace, understanding, and cooperation, especially in the present world situation which is extremely tense and complicated.[24]

WCC leaders met again with Eastern European church representatives in Budapest in January of 1980. These talks centered on the increased participation in WCC affairs by churches from the Eastern bloc. Also highlighted was the increase in the number of Eastern Europeans serving on the WCC staff, and the rise in the number of WCC-sponsored meetings held in Eastern European countries. An agreement was reached that Eastern European churches should be more involved in planning the 1983 WCC Assembly at Vancouver than they had been in preparing the 1975 Assembly at Nairobi.[25]

In the eight years between the Nairobi and Vancouver Assemblies, numerous ecumenical leaders visited Eastern Europe. For example, Paul Hansen of the Lutheran World Federation (LWF) visited the Soviet Union and upon his return declared that "idealizing unrecognized religious groups in the Soviet Union would be unjust to the many faithful Christians who want to practice their belief within the laws of the State."[26] Representatives of the WCC, the Conference of European Churches (CEC), and several American churches often consulted with Russian Orthodox church leaders on a variety of subjects. In May of 1976, the CEC's Presidium and Advisory Committee, which includes churches in both Eastern and Western Europe, met in Moscow. Its emphasis was a familiar one: that churches' concerns for human rights ought not to be addressed apart from other international issues.[27] Another CEC meeting was held in Moscow in 1983 and received favorable coverage from the Soviet press. [28] Then, the CCIA held its regional meeting in Kiev in June of 1979, arriving at positions that largely conformed to official Soviet policies.

A prime instrument throughout these years in promoting the Soviet Union's foreign policy goals was the Prague-based Christian Peace Conference (CPC). The CPC exerts considerable influence on ecumenical affairs because many of its leaders are members of the WCC's Central Committee or other important Council bodies. At a meeting with Potter and WCC staff in 1982, Bishop Karoly Toth, who succeeded Nikodim as leader of the CPC, said the Conference would make significant contributions to the forthcoming Vancouver Assembly. Potter and CPC leaders agreed at the same meeting to explore ways in which cooperation between the WCC and CPC could be broadened. [29]

Of Yakunin: "No action contemplated"

The developing relationship between WCC leaders and representatives of Eastern bloc churches was not without its problems. Part of the difficulty was the WCC's obsession with smoothing over the Yakunin-Regelson "incident" at Nairobi by trying to create an impression of harmony and friendship with Eastern bloc governments. As a result, WCC criticism of Eastern bloc governments was rendered all but impossible. The Council's determination to make pronouncements on international issues in cooperation with representatives of churches essentially captive to totalitarian governments had its inevitable consequences. As Dutch theologian J.A. Hebly has said:

> Most churches in Eastern Europe have no possibility of taking an independent stance in regard to national political issues. Their peace work is nothing more than amplifying the points of view of their government—with the important exception of the churches in the German Democratic Republic and Poland. [30]

The Russian Orthodox church, for example, because it is controlled by the Soviet government, cannot invite the WCC to address religious rights or any other issues concerning Christians in the Soviet Union. [31] The Soviet government occasionally permits the Russian Orthodox church to intervene on behalf of the individuals under arrest or in prison, but it is possible that this is a propaganda device to suggest a certain independence for the Russian church. An example of this phenomenon was the WCC's successful

19

appeal, through the Russian Orthodox church, on behalf of the so-called "Siberian Seven," who were seven Pentecostal families that sought refuge in the U.S. Embassy in Moscow in 1978.[32]

On the whole, however, the Moscow Patriarchate of the Russian Orthodox church rarely defends clerics when the Soviet government seeks their transfer or even dismissal. Nor did the Patriarchate attempt to prevent the Soviet government's arrest in November 1979 of Father Gleb Yakunin, the priest whose letter had caused such a stir at the Nairobi Assembly four years earlier. In 1976 Yakunin had founded the "Christian Committee for the Defense of Believers' Rights in the USSR" because, he said, the Russian Orthodox bishops and other church leaders "do not concern themselves with the defense of believers' rights."[33] Among the work of Yakunin's Committee was an August 1979 report entitled "On the Current Situation of the Russian Orthodox Church and Perspectives on the Religious Revival in Russia." The Committee report claimed to prove that the Soviet government has virtual control over the official Orthodox church, and recommended formation of truly independent Christian communities.

For these endeavors, Yakunin was arrested by Soviet authorities on charges of "anti-Soviet agitation and propaganda." The trial began on 25 August 1980. After testimony that his letter to the Nairobi Assembly had adversely affected the Russian church's reputation in other countries, Yakunin was sentenced to five years in prison, to be followed by five years of internal exile. Lev Regelson, the layman who had signed the letter to the Nairobi Assembly with Yakunin, was also arrested, but was released after pleading guilty to similar charges.

The WCC made no statement on the Yakunin trial. When the Council's Central Committee met in Geneva in August of 1980, it received "with appreciation" a CCIA report on religious liberty, but it offered no comment on the Yakunin case—which went to trial that very month.[34] The only WCC reactions were a few mild letters from the CCIA to Russian Orthodox church leaders in keeping with the Council's policy of silent diplomacy.

The WCC's silence about Yakunin did not go without notice or protest. Michael Bourdeaux, director of Keston College, a research institute near London, called on the Council to issue a public declaration on behalf of both Yakunin and Regelson. Keston, in cooperation with two other research institutions, had presented to the WCC's Central Committee in 1976 a well-documented report on "Religious Liberty in the Soviet Union." Bourdeaux's efforts proved unsuccessful. An appeal sent by Bourdeaux to CCIA Director

Leopoldo Niilus, received a terse reply: "Re Yakunin. At present no action contemplated."

But Bourdeaux was undeterred; he carried his protest to the British church and public, as he later explained:

> I thought, here is a man (Yakunin) who should be one of the leaders of the ecumenical movement, because of its concern for worldwide Christianity, and the WCC will do nothing to help him. So I didn't waste any time on further telexes. I made a public statement and sent it to the Anglican newspaper *Church Times* and to the BBC. *Church Times* published it, and the BBC took it up as well. I had a debate with a WCC staff member in Geneva over the radio. As a result of my challenge to the WCC (though they will never admit this is what happened) they wrote a letter to the Russian church expressing their concern about the trials of Christians.[35]

The letter to which Bourdeaux refers was sent by the WCC's acting general secretary, Konrad Raiser, to Metropolitan Yuvenaliy, chairman of the Russian Orthodox church's foreign affairs department, on 1 October 1980. Raiser wrote of his concern about the trials of Yakunin and Regelson, and also about the trials of Dimitri Dudko and other Russian Christians: "We find the kind of sentence pronounced in the trials already concluded to be disproportionate with the seriousness of the crimes which have allegedly been committed." He concluded by asking the Russian Orthodox church to "convey our concerns to the highest relevant authorities."[36]

It was a sign of some change that the WCC could be prompted (albeit reluctantly) to send such a letter to Russian Orthodox officials and, through them, to Soviet authorities. After all, under Nikodim, who was Yuvenaliy's predecessor in the Moscow Patriarchate, such concerns about human rights in the Soviet Union could not be publicly addressed at all. But Yuvenaliy's reply to Raiser's letter added some offsetting points:

> With regard to your remarks as to the severity of the verdicts, I am obliged to draw your attention to the fact that in all instances where the accused admitted their guilt and showed repentance, leniency was granted to them in the eyes of the law. This applies both to Fr. Dimitri Dudko and to Lev Regelson's case. Fr. Dimitri Dudko has already been appointed by me to serve in my own diocese, which is the closest to Moscow...although the investigation of his case is not yet complete.[37]

In other words, Yakunin, Regelson and Dudko were still regarded as criminals who had to admit their "guilt" and "repent" when they had done nothing but exercise the freedom of expression guaranteed in international codes to human rights. The Soviet constitution guarantees freedom of speech only so long as it is "in accordance with the interests of the people and with a view to strengthening the socialist order."

Although Yuvenaliy's response may show at least some evidence that state control of the church was lessening in the Soviet Union, the truth is probably that both church and state officials in the Soviet Union realized that remaining in good standing with the worldwide ecumenical community—especially on issues pertaining to "peace"—involved certain concessions. On occasion, this might require a bow, at least, to ecumenical pressure for some leniency.

The Vancouver Assembly, 1983

The question of religious freedom in the Soviet Union probably arose before the 1983 Vancouver Assembly in meetings between high WCC officials and leaders of the Russian Orthodox church. For example, a few months before the Assembly was scheduled to convene, a meeting took place between Potter and Archbishop Edward W. Scott, moderator of the WCC's Central Committee, and Patriach Pimen and other Russian Orthodox officials.[38] Potter also visited the Russian church's foreign affairs department where he met with Metropolitan Filaret, who directs this office and who later led the Russian delegation to Vancouver. At the time, Filaret was directly involved in a Soviet-sponsored "peace offensive" against the West.[39]

A likely topic of discussion at these meetings was a mutual determination to keep the kind of disruption caused at Nairobi eight years earlier by the Yakunin-Regelson letter from repeating itself at Vancouver. On the same day that he visited the Russian Orthodox church's foreign affairs office, Potter met with three high officials of the Soviet government's Council for Religious Affairs. These meetings may explain why the WCC leadership refused to allow discussion at Vancouver of an open letter to delegates from Vladimir Rusak, a deacon in the Russian Orthodox church.

In his plea to the Vancouver Assembly, Rusak described a church controlled by the Soviet government:

The aim of the Soviet authorities in using the church is purely propagandistic. It helps increase the political dividends reaped by the authorities on the international scene and rationalizes the continued existence of the church in a socialist state, as the interchurch and international activity of our church's representatives is directed first and foremost, to serve the interests of the secular (i.e., Soviet-atheist) regime to the detriment of the interests of the church and all the faithful.[40]

The WCC, Rusak declared, should cease "to identify the Soviet delegation at international gatherings with the whole body of the Russian Orthodox Church." "[Our]) hope [is] that the WCC will stop treating the propagandistic claims of Soviet delegates as the only source of information." Rusak also urged that religious freedom be discussed openly. The Yakunin-Regelson letter at the Nairobi Assembly had "yielded some definite results," he said, citing "hurried publication of the Bible which had been awaited by millions of believers for many years."[41]

Rusak had been dismissed by his church's leadership from his position as a deacon when he refused to destroy a report he had prepared about the history of the Russian Orthodox church after the 1917 Russian Revolution. The KGB confiscated the report, but not before a copy had been smuggled to the West. In it, Rusak maintains that the Soviet government deliberately keeps the Soviet people uninformed of the real condition of the church: "Obviously, it is easier to manage an ignorant mass of people (albeit a believing one) than an informed one."

Presumably as a result of the Yakunin-Regelson letter, WCC staff at Vancouver were instructed not to publish letters by dissidents from the Soviet Union. In addition, staff suppressed a letter on behalf of thirty-five imprisoned Christians and 20,000 Pentecostals who wanted to emigrate from the Soviet Union—a letter prepared by the "Christian Committee for the Defense of Believers' Rights in the Soviet Union"—the group founded by Yakunin in 1976.

Ninan Koshy, who succeeded Leopoldo Niilius as CCIA director in 1981, explained this policy at a press conference at Vancouver: "Appeals from groups or individuals for World Council of Churches' intervention cannot be acted on by the Assembly without the support of delegates of member churches, but will be followed up by the WCC general secretary."[42]

By this statement, Koshy could not have meant that the WCC does not criticize certain governments for alleged violations of human rights. Koshy himself in March of 1982 sent a telegram to President Ferdinand Marcos of the Philippines, protesting the Marcos government's arrest of several Christians.[43] At Vancouver, Koshy was really expressing the WCC's decision to not directly address alleged human rights violations by the Soviet government, even when members of the state-sanctioned Russian Orthodox church were involved.

This apparent double standard surfaced often at the Vancouver Assembly. For example, the WCC issued a broad call for the church to be vigilant on behalf of human rights. The Assembly resolved that it is "imperative that member churches and the WCC continue to identify and denounce gross violations of religious freedom and extend moral and material assistance to those who suffer oppression and even persecution because of their religious beliefs and practices."[44] This appears in the Assembly's lengthy "Statement on Human Rights," which also notes that "many persons, including Christians and their leaders, have been imprisoned, tortured, or have lost their lives in service to God and humanity." The statement adds that "the violations of human rights in many parts of the world have become more widespread and severe," and chides churches which "have not done enough to counter the forces of evil and death, at times even being in complicity with them."[45]

Although such a statement can be construed as a rebuke of Eastern bloc governments, the Assembly effectively undercut that interpretation:

> We have also come to appreciate more clearly the complexity and interrelatedness of human rights. In this regard we recognize the need to set individual rights and their violation in the context of society and its social structures.
>
> We are increasingly aware of the fact that human rights cannot be dealt with in isolation from the larger issues of peace, justice, militarism, disarmament and development.[46]

This concept emphasizes "collective human rights" which obscures authentic concerns for human rights by endless discussions of social, economic and political issues. Distinctly Eastern bloc in origin and nature, its adoption by the World Council of Churches is additional testimony to the organization's unwillingness to really confront the question of religious repression in the Soviet Union.

More recently, some in the WCC claim credit for the changes and reforms in Soviet society which have followed Mikhail Gorbachev's ascent to power. In view of the WCC's past questionable role in dealing with human rights issues in Communist bloc countries, such claims seem hardly justified. Indeed, in years past the Soviet government successfully manipulated WCC leaders on many occasions and it is likely to do so under Gorbachev.

Current Soviet reforms may very well be due to other factors, notably Western resolve vis-á-vis Soviet policies with respect to Eastern Europe, Afghanistan or the nuclear missile issue. The Soviets under Gorbachev have obviously come to appreciate this. It was not quite coincidental that Soviet leader Mikhail Gorbachev first sought consensus with Western leaders like Margaret Thatcher and President Reagan—often portrayed as conservative in WCC circles.

Monitoring
Human Rights in Asia

Hanoi, Saigon and the WCC

In 1973, two years before South Vietnam fell to the North Vietnamese army, the WCC's "Commission on World Mission and Evangelism" asked the North Vietnamese government in Hanoi to receive an international delegation of church leaders to express solidarity with those who had been "terrorized" by American bombing. The request typified the WCC's attitude toward the war. The WCC consistently refused to recognize (and still does today) that North Vietnam, and not only the United States, contributed to the political and military problems of Indochina. The continued U.S. military presence in Vietnam, the Council states, "whether through 'Vietnamization,' the air war, or in any form, is detrimental to the peace in Indochina."[1] The Council condemned U.S. and South Vietnamese military operations in Laos and Cambodia, even though the strikes were launched against North Vietnamese military bases in those two neighboring countries, which were being used as bases to attack South Vietnamese and American troops in South Vietnam. Yet the Council was relatively silent about the earlier North Vietnamese operations in Laos and Cambodia that had provoked the South Vietnamese and American retaliation.

So, too, when the "Agreement on Ending the War and Restoring Peace in Vietnam" was signed between North Vietnam and South Vietnam at Paris in January of 1973, many WCC officials tended to see things from Hanoi's perspective, not Saigon's. A few months after the conclusion of the Paris Agreement, the WCC's Commission on International Affairs (CCIA) condemned the government of South Vietnam for not releasing political prisoners, but made no mention of political detainees in North Vietnam. While South Vietnam was rightly expected "to release all political prisoners, and to immediately restore the democratic liberties for which the Agreement provides," the CCIA simply assumed that North Vietnam had already met these conditions.[2]

The subsequent North Vietnamese invasion of South Vietnam in March 1975 also occasioned little WCC response. Ecumenical leaders had specifically condemned North Korean aggression in 1950, but in 1975 the Council's Executive Committee, meeting in Geneva shortly before the collapse of the South Vietnamese government, produced only a mild statement appealing "to the signatories (of the Paris Agreement) to comply with its provisions, especially those which call for the restoration of democratic liberties." The Executive Committee also:

> ...urged all states outside Vietnam to refrain from any military involvement or presence in South Vietnam, and encouraged the United States in accordance with the terms of the Agreement to resist pressures to provide further military aid to the Saigon government.[3]

"Outside Vietnam"? The implication was clear: The WCC's executive committee deemed the United States to be "the aggressor" in Vietnam—not the Vietnamese Communists headquartered in Hanoi who had waged war against the people of South Vietnam.

The Statement hardly touched upon the tragedy that had befallen the hundreds of thousands of people who had attempted to escape Communist occupation of the South. The WCC Statement simply noted "that the majority of people have remained in their places as control of territory has changed."[4] There was no recognition that people facing a Communist takeover might prefer fleeing rather than living under Communism. Indeed, when Cambodia and Laos fell to pro-Communist forces in the same year, the WCC continued to view these developments as only the internal affairs of the states concerned.

Vietnam after Paris

Between 1975 and 1978, the human rights situation in Vietnam deteriorated rapidly. Much has been written about the brutal "Hanoization" of South Vietnam, the use of "yellow rain" against Laotian tribesmen, the mass detentions without trial, and the "reeducation" camps. Even as late as 1983, Vietnam held thousands of political prisoners—perhaps as many as 126,000, according to the Human Rights Working Group within the European Parliament.[5] Vietnamese from the South also were sent to Siberia where they were forced to work for the Soviets, usually under harsh conditions.[6]

Most striking, perhaps, was the plight of the so-called "boat people." They were refugees, principally from Vietnam, but also from Cambodia and Laos, who were fleeing Communist expansion in Indochina. They numbered in the hundreds of thousands—200,000 in 1979 alone—and their stories are horrifying. Untold thousands died at sea.[7]

There also have been serious allegations of persecution in Vietnam of religious individuals and churches, notably Catholic and Buddhist. Repression of religious activities began in 1976 and by August of the same year religious freedom was severely curtailed; hundreds of Catholic priests throughout the former South Vietnam were arrested, and others were harassed.[8]

Many Catholics and Buddhists who had previously welcomed the Communist takeover were shocked at being arrested and subsequently transferred to reeducation camps. A number of Catholic priests died as a result of ill-treatment during detention. Christian communities in the Central Highlands were relocated by force; children were taken from their parents for Communist indoctrination.

There are still churches in Vietnam, maintained, by and large, for propaganda purposes. Provided they are subservient to the government, Vietnamese religious leaders are allowed to travel—to propagate government policies at so-called "peace conferences" in both the West and the East. But there is no freedom "to criticize the ruling powers when necessary," which the Nairobi Assembly of the WCC in December 1975 recognized as "the right and duty of religious bodies."[9]

The WCC has preferred to remain silent on these issues. When in September 1976 a trial of fourteen dissidents ended in death sentences for three of the defendants—including a Roman Catholic priest—the WCC didn't make a sound.[10] Instead, addressing the Sixth General Assembly of the Christian Conference of Asia (CCA), WCC General Secretary Philip Potter praised the Vietnamese:

The experience of the Vietnamese people has inspired all who fight for liberation. The victory of the Vietnamese ended thirty years of the most destructive war the world has ever seen. The most dramatic manifestation of the hope of our time was given by the Vietnamese people.[11]

29

At the 1975 Nairobi Assembly, a document on "Structures of Injustice and Struggles for Liberation" was careful to skirt the question of Indochina. An amendment that called attention to "the one-party states in the People's Republic of China, North Korea, Vietnam, Cambodia, and Laos" as among the governments violating human rights was squashed by those —principally the influential Metropolitan Paulos Mar Gregorios of India— who criticized the assumption that a one-party state is necessarily evil.[12] The amendment was redrafted as follows:

> Many changes are taking place in Asian governments. There is martial law in Taiwan; crisis government in the Philippines; emergency rule in India and South Korea; military rule in Bangladesh; one-party states in such countries as the People's Republic of China. In all the other countries of Asia (e.g., Malaysia, Singapore, Australia, New Zealand, Indonesia, and Japan) there are also violations of human rights. Whenever human rights are suppressed or violated by any Asian government, churches have a duty to work for the defense of human rights especially of the oppressed. We believe that the whole mission of the church is involved in this issue and urge churches to work for the right of the people of Asia to participate in their own development.[13]

Somehow the names of Vietnam, Laos and Cambodia were left out of the final text as adopted by the Assembly. Apparently the WCC believed that "structures of injustice" had been eradicated in these areas and recognized new "structures of liberation" in their place.

Earlier, the WCC's "Salvation Today" Conference at Bangkok, Thailand, in 1973, had linked "salvation" to the "peace of the people in Vietnam."[14] Now that there was "peace" in Vietnam, salvation had evidently been realized.

The WCC, equally evasive on the question of Cambodia, avoided a public statement on the deteriorating human rights situation there at the Central Committee meeting in August of 1976. General Secretary Philip Potter was embarrassed when journalists fired questions at him during a press conference shortly before the Central Committee convened. Reports of mass killings in Cambodia had widely circulated in the West and were taken seriously by most Western governments and secular news media, particularly in Europe. Potter obviously did not like the questions on Cambodia posed to him, and lamely explained:

The question is not whether or not any Cambodians have been killed, but how one could create the proper atmosphere in order to raise issues through "personal contacts." There is too much self-righteousness on such issues. We should first of all take our own situation into account. We are all sinners.[15]

Potter had not been so complacent about the American bombing of Vietnam a few years earlier.

Another WCC excuse for not making many public statements about Cambodia was that there were hardly any Christian churches there. The WCC, it was urged, "is not a human rights organization, neither does it make statements merely for the purpose of improving its own public image."[16] But, after Vietnam had installed a sympathetic regime in Phnom Penh, and started revealing some of the atrocities committed in Cambodia between 1975 and 1978 by the previous regime, the WCC began to devote more attention to those mass killings. In 1980, the Central Committee was belatedly informed of these massacres by a fifteen minute slides/tape presentation "illustrating the disaster which in recent years had engulfed the people of Kampuchea."[17] Yet nothing had changed except that the Vietnamese had a vested interest in making the Khmer Rouge atrocities as widely known as possible in order to justify their own armed intervention.

In other words, it is difficult to escape the conclusion that during this period the WCC policy toward Indochina was motivated less by humanitarian concern than by a sympathy with certain political agendas. At the 1979 Central Committee meeting in Jamaica, discussion of Indochina was brief and dispassionate. The adopted text read simply:

The consequences of thirty years of war in Indochina are still being felt. Alliances involving the USA, the USSR, China, and the Indochinese nations add new aspects to existing international conflicts in the area. The churches and the WCC should keep this situation under constant review. In light of the escalation between Vietnam and Cambodia, and its possible implications for the area as a whole, urgent special attention is required on this particular matter. The CCIA should seek to provide, within its possibilities, objective information about the nature of these respective national situations and the regional context.[18]

Responding to the request of the Central Committee, the WCC's

Commission on International Affairs produced a booklet on the Indochina conflict that same year. It described the period in Indochina from 1975 "as one of consolidation and intensive reconstruction,"[19] a view virtually indistinguishable from official Vietnamese propaganda which stressed "socialist solidarity" and the need for rapid reconstruction under Vietnamese control. The stability of the region, the WCC report said, "depends on two related factors: the situation in Kampuchea and the extent of socialist solidarity among the three Indochinese countries. The sporadic guerrilla warfare in Kampuchea and the recognition question on the diplomatic front contribute to the current instability."[20]

The same WCC that was later to denounce American and East Caribbean intervention in Grenada as a violation of international law made no public statement condemning the Vietnamese intervention in Cambodia. A WCC delegation visiting Vietnam, Laos and Cambodia in January of 1981 concluded that, "if all roads in Indochina now lead to Hanoi, that is more by force of circumstances and pressure from countries outside the region than by any deliberate plans for an Indochinese federation...The strategy of denial at present followed by Western nations and their Asian allies will only prolong the conflicts in the region."[21] Blame thus fell on every head other than that of Vietnam.

Aiding Indochinese Refugees

There was a refugee problem in Indochina even before the Communist takeovers in South Vietnam, Laos and Cambodia in 1975. To deal with that problem, the WCC's Commission on Inter-church Aid, Refugee, and World Service (CICARWS), had created in 1972 a special "Fund for Reconstruction and Reconciliation in Indochina."

The Fund had a pro-Hanoi bias, and its first major ecumenical consultation, "Reconstruction and Reconciliation in Indochina," in February 1975 concerned itself exclusively with alleged American and South Vietnamese violations of the Paris Agreement and ignored charges against North Vietnam and the Provisional Revolutionary Government of South Vietnam.[22]

When the refugee problem took a dramatic turn for the worse after 1975, the WCC—while fully concerned about the new problem—never explicitly abandoned the pro-Hanoi bias of its earlier aid efforts or acknowledged that North Vietnam had largely caused the whole problem. In 1979, for example, the refugee problem had reached such vast proportions that WCC General Secretary Philip Potter sent a message to the general secretary of the United Nations, Kurt Waldheim, urging him "to have further discussions with the Vietnamese government for measures that would avoid undue hardship and danger for those who leave the country." But Potter's letter focused only on effects, not causes. He urged WCC churches to bring pressure on their governments, especially in affluent countries, to accept more refugees from Indochina.[23]

Similarly, in Dresden during August 1981, the Central Committee received a document prepared by CICARWS on "The Churches and the World Refugee Crisis," which began:

A worldwide refugee disaster of unprecedented proportions is fast developing, a cumulative nightmare for many millions of men, women, and children forced to flee their homes. Whole populations have become refugees from war, repression, or deprivation. Semi-permanent concentrations of refugees continue to accumulate in several parts of the world, but they risk being forgotten as newer refugee movements claim priority.[24]

A statement on the "World Refugee Crisis" was adopted and, after debate, an amendment urging "governments to respect the security and territorial integrity of countries which are hosts of refugees" was incorporated into the draft text.[25] But when a delegate observed that the basic cause of the refugee problem had been overlooked, the point was allowed only in its most general application: people became refugees when they were deprived of their basic human rights, therefore governments should see to it that those rights were respected.[26] No specific government was identified, and subsequent WCC criticism of human rights infringements in Vietnam, Cambodia and Laos was very restrained.

In other refugee situations, WCC staff members would readily name the culprits. For example, the Migration secretary of the WCC, Alan Matheson, strongly criticized those governments he held responsible for "the other boat people," those from Haiti. This "tragedy in the history of the oppressed people of Haiti" was caused by "the cynicism of the United States government, the brutality of some Caribbean governments, the oppression of the Duvalier dictatorship together with the apathy of the world community."[27]

But the WCC would never be so blunt on Indochina. There, WCC aid concentrated not only on refugees, but also on development projects in Laos, Vietnam and Cambodia. As a result, the WCC had a stake in those governments; Council efforts were, in effect, instrumental in consolidating Vietnamese power in the region. The ties were more than economic, they were personal. The Vietnamese government always insisted on having good relations with both the WCC and the American churches, and the churches responded in kind. This made it even more difficult for the WCC to honestly criticize the Vietnamese government.

The two Chinas

The WCC exonerated Communist governments while repeatedly denouncing pro-Western governments throughout East Asia. For example, the WCC has seldom disapproved of conditions in the People's Republic of China (PRC) and was among the first organizations to insist on China's admission to the United Nations. The brutal repression during the Cultural Revolution was not a matter of major concern. Even so, there were many elements within the WCC that sympathized with the "Chinese experience," and described it as a model society. In a statement entitled "The World Council of Churches and China," the WCC's Commission on World Mission and Evangelism (CWME) meeting in Bangkok in 1973 emphasized "the need for a theological and ethical understanding of the transformation of Chinese society and its implications for other societies."[28] There were even those among the ecumenical elite who compared Maoism to the realization of the Kingdom of God.[29]

The WCC did not even respond to an urgent 1978 Amnesty International report on "Political Imprisonment in the People's Republic of China." The rationale of the Council's attitude seemed to be that to do so would be an affront to churches and Christians in China with whom it preferred to have the best relations possible. One such Chinese Christian was Bishop K.H. Ting of Nanking, who had consistently supported the Chinese government.

Nor was anything heard from the WCC when, in the late 1970s, the Chinese government suppressed a dissident movement. One of the dissidents, Wei Jingsheng, had edited the independent journal *Tansuo*. After he had written a detailed description of the Chinese prison system and its methods of torture, he was arrested on 29 March 1979. Parts of his sensational trial were shown on Chinese television.[30]

The fate of dissidents in non-Communist Asian countries, however, was a different story. The WCC was very vocal about restrictions on religious freedom in the Republic of China (Taiwan). The WCC had particularly strong ties with the Presbyterian Church of Taiwan (PCT), which consists largely of native Taiwanese who have opposed the Kuo

Min-Tang domination since the beginning. Kuo Min-Tang rule was imposed on the native Taiwanese when the remnant of General Chiang Kai-shek's forces escaped the Communist takeover in China by fleeing to the few islands where the Communists had not yet assumed power and were unlikely to do so in the near future.

In the course of time, however, tensions between the native population and the rulers began to manifest themselves. The PCT had a serious clash with the government in 1970 after it called for the admission of the People's Republic of China into the United Nations. This was particularly an affront to the government, since, so far, the Chinese seat within the United Nations had been occupied by the Republic of China or Taiwan.

The PCT participated in the mass demonstration of Taiwanese opposition groups on Human Rights Day in December of 1979. Among those later arrested in the "Kaohsiung" incident were PCT members including the church's general secretary. The WCC responded quickly. In April of 1980, WCC General Secretary Potter sent a telegram to President Chiang Ching-Kuo of Taiwan which read:

> [The] World Council of Churches expresses its great shock and grave concern at [the] arrest of Reverend Kao, General Secretary [of the] Presbyterian Church [of] Taiwan. Christians in all parts of [the] world hold him in great esteem. We urge his immediate release.[31]

Then, in May, a delegation of the WCC and the World Alliance of Reformed Churches (WARC) paid a visit to Taiwan to protest Kao's arrest and to express solidarity with the PCT:

> We regret that we must report that to Christian observers in other parts of the world, it appears that when the Presbyterian Church of Taiwan began to articulate the relevance of the Christian Gospel to their daily life in this society, that church and its leaders became the objects of persecution. Freedom of religion means more than simply the freedom of worship; it means freedom to live out the implications of one's faith as well.[32]

"Silent Diplomacy" in the Koreas and the Philippines

The WCC also seemed to apply a double standard to human rights in Korea. The Republic of South Korea, not the Communist government of North Korea, has taken the brunt of criticism. In 1979, for example, a CCIA report both denounced the human rights situation in South Korea and denied that any improvement was taking place. As for North Korea, where, according to independent sources such as Freedom House, human rights abuses are worse than in South Korea, the same report had little to say. As CCIA Director Leopoldo Niilus wrote:

The publication of this report is not without risks. Similar publications have in the past been used as propaganda tools of North Korea, with the consequent labelling by South Korean authorities of its authors as Communist agitators. Indeed, the extremely limited information which is available about the human rights behavior of the Democratic People's Republic of Korea does not suggest it as a valid candidate for an alternative. Those who are struggling for democracy in South Korea clearly posit that both regimes must be democratized before reunification talks can become fruitful.[33]

Obviously, this was said to explain the WCC's silence on the human rights situation in North Korea where there are large numbers of political prisoners and torture is reportedly common.

The WCC has also been vigilant about human rights practices in the Philippines. In September of 1977, Potter sent a cable appealing to President Marcos "to grant general and unconditional amnesty to all political prisoners and to restore the human rights and fundamental freedoms of the people."[34] Potter also protested the "suppression of people's movements struggling for social and economic justice." In November 1980 WCC acting General Secretary Konrad Raiser devoted special attention to the arrest and detention of Senator Jovito Salonga, a member of the WCC's Commission on International Affairs.[35] These actions were, of course, legitimate, because there were many human rights violations under the Marcos regime. But sometimes a telling note creeps into WCC directives. For example, Council spokesmen more than once criticized the U.S. military presence in the Philippines. According to Niilus, "the perspective of the victims of militarization on the Philippines" is different from those who make U.S. policy. "The national security argument is an insult to the people whose security is in peril." There is a "direct correlation between militarization and human rights" as there is also a link between "numerous transnational corporations and militarization."[36]

The Vancouver Assembly of 1983 referred to "the negative effects of the continuation of U.S. military bases in the Philippines. The presence of these foreign conventional and nuclear forces poses a threat to the sovereignty, security, and human rights of the Filipino people." The Assembly asked the Council's general secretary "to recommend to the churches appropriate actions in support of the churches in the Philippines and the efforts of the Filipino people for the withdrawal of the bases."[37]

American churches which hold the same view and have pressured the American government to withdraw from the Philippines are given all the moral and political support they require.

The WCC appears to hold that the United States, through its military presence in the Philippines, contributes to a policy of repression. There is no recognition that American administrations have repeatedly pressed for human rights and that, in view of its special ties with the Philippine government, the United States has been in a unique position to do so.

It seems that the WCC reserves to itself the right of "silent diplomacy," and denies the privilege to the governments for which it has consistently expressed a dislike. Indeed, without substantial American pressure, President Marcos would not have stepped down in February of 1986 when he hesitated to relinquish power after Mrs. Corazon Aquino won an historic election to the Philippine presidency. Paradoxically, it was the Soviets, not the Americans, who supported Marcos in the final days of his government, when it appeared he might try to retain rule. On 19 February the new Soviet ambassador to the Philippines became the first and only envoy from a major foreign government to congratulate Marcos on his "reelection."[38]

"Threats to Peace":
Conflict and Compromise

The Afghan crisis

In December 1979 Soviet armed forces invaded neighboring Afghanistan, ostensibly at the request of Afghanistan's pro-Soviet government whose president Hafizullah Amin was killed by Soviet elite forces even before he could make such a request. Many governments around the world responded immediately and protested. In the United States, the U.S. Senate refused to approve the SALT II Treaty. Worldwide protests of the invasion heightened as hundreds of thousands of Afghans fled to nearby Pakistan and as clashes intensified between Afghan resistance fighters and Soviet troops assisted by Afghan Army forces.

The World Council of Churches waited nearly two months before one of its bodies commented on the Soviet incursion. In February of 1980, the WCC's Executive Committee included a reference to "the military action by the USSR in Afghanistan" in a statement entitled "Threats to Peace." The document called the invasion "the latest direct, armed intervention in one country by another," and said it had "heightened the tension, especially in and around the area of development."[1] The WCC has played a significant role in assisting church-sponsored work among Afghan refugees in Pakistan and elsewhere, but the Council's position on the political issues in Afghanistan has been quite another matter.

The WCC has previously responded more readily and emphatically to armed invasions. For example, when North Korean troops invaded South Korea in 1950, the WCC's Central Committee immediately denounced the attack: "An act of aggression has been committed. The United Nations

Commission in Korea, the most objective witness available, asserts that 'all evidence points to a calculated, coordinated attack prepared and launched with secrecy' by the North Korean troops."[2] The WCC statement was severely criticized by churches from Communist countries. Dr. T.C. Chao of the People's Republic of China—Communist China—even resigned as WCC president in protest. It was only after the influential Russian Orthodox church joined the WCC in 1961 that the Council gradually began to change its views toward policies of the Soviet Union. The Soviet government had strongly favored Russian Orthodox participation in the WCC which it sought to manipulate through a church fully under its control.[3]

When Soviet troops crushed the Czechoslovakian Prague Spring movement in August of 1968, the officers of the WCC had immediately issued a statement of concern about "this ill-considered action by the USSR and its allies." The same statement appealed "to the government of the USSR to reconsider the policy which dictated the military intervention, to remove all its troops from Czechoslovakia at the earliest possible moment, and to renounce the use of force or threat upon its allies."[4]

But in 1980, the WCC's Executive Committee produced a statement which only partially dealt with the Afghanistan issue. Some had pressed for a separate statement on Afghanistan, but the Committee as a whole could only, in a compromise, link the Soviet military intervention to other "threats to peace." These included, in the Committee's perspective, the decision to deploy cruise and Pershing II missiles in Europe by the United States and NATO in December 1979.

"No single event should be seen in isolation," the Council's statement on Afghanistan declared. Moreover, unlike the WCC comment on the Soviet action in Czechoslovakia in 1968, the pronouncement on Afghanistan did not call on the Soviets to withdraw their troops "at the earliest possible moment."

The "Threats to Peace" compromise resulted from a serious debate among two major points of view among WCC member churches. On one hand were those who insisted that the Soviet invasion of Afghanistan was the most serious current threat to worldwide peace; on the other hand were those who contended that the fighting in Afghanistan should not be considered apart from other international issues—especially policies of the United States and NATO. Promoting this latter viewpoint was the Russian Orthodox church, which was represented on the WCC's Executive Committee by Archbishop Kirill of Leningrad. He maintained that there was a direct link between the Soviet action in Afghanistan and NATO's decision of December 1979 to deploy new nuclear missiles in Europe. In addition, Kirill argued that the Soviet government had responded to the specific request of the Afghan government, which he said faced outside aggression.

Neither side prevailed entirely in the WCC deliberations. Kirill compromised by agreeing to a statement that called the Soviet invasion a "threat to peace" and ranked it ahead of six other international issues about which the WCC expressed "serious concern." Others agreed to link the Soviet invasion to NATO's missile deployment, and by yielding on their earlier request that the WCC would produce a statement solely dealing with Afghanistan. The resulting compromise was unanimously approved by the Executive Committee.

However, the WCC decision did not end the matter. Kirill soon found himself criticized by some for not resisting strongly enough the efforts to condemn the Soviet invasion. On 20 March 1980, the Holy Synod of the Russian Orthodox church endorsed what it called the "assistance" given to the Afghan government by troops of the Soviet Union:

> We, churchmen, understand and accept the reasons which prompted the Soviet government to take such a step, and we by no means recognize as justifiable the use of the Afghan events by the USA and other countries to forcefully intensify tension in the relations between East and West, between the USSR and some non-European countries.[5]

Thereafter, any attempt at gaining a WCC condemnation of the Soviet invasion of Afghanistan would be frustrated.

The debate at Melbourne, May 1980

The first major WCC meeting after the "Threats to Peace" statement was the World Conference on Missions and Evangelism held in Melbourne in May 1980. Its theme, "Your Kingdom Come," lent itself to political interpretations and uses. The meeting focused on a "theology of the poor and oppressed" as an extension of the "theology of liberation." The Kingdom of God was declared to be manifest mainly (though not exclusively) in human struggles for "liberation."[6] Despite ardent dissent by delegates holding the traditional view of the biblical kingdom, and of the WCC's purposes, the Melbourne meeting was charged with political overtones.

41

Its lengthy "Declaration on the Situation in El Salvador and Latin America," for example, accepted the political premises of liberation theology.[7]

It seemed to be quite easy for the Conference to adopt the slogan "Stop the Repression in El Salvador!" Once again, however, the WCC was unable to adopt any official statement concerning a repression far more severe than any in El Salvador—the repression of the entire country of Afghanistan by Soviet forces. Aided by churches from some Latin American countries, the Russian Orthodox church was able to thwart any such attempts.

Paradoxically, American delegates to the Melbourne conference played a part in excluding the invasion of Afghanistan from policy consider-ations. At their own initiative, delegations of several American churches invited the Soviet Union delegations to an evening meeting to discuss the churches' role as "agents of reconciliation." At this meeting, the Ameri-cans and Russians agreed to exclude the Soviet invasion from confer-ence deliberations, and to concentrate on issues less divisive, including the churches' role in proclaiming peace.[8]

A similar agreement had been made at the Nairobi Assembly in 1975 between Russian Orthodox church delegates and representatives of church-es in the Third World, especially Latin America. On that occasion, the agreement was for Third World delegates to refrain from opposing the nomination of Metropolitan Nikodim, head of the Russian Orthodox church delegation, as a WCC president.[9]

Despite such efforts, it was not easy for delegates at Melbourne to avoid discussing the Soviet invasion of Afghanistan. Many raised the issue. They pointed out that the draft text of "The Kingdom of God and Human Struggles" paper mentioned specific regions and countries where strug-gles for freedom were taking place. As Dutch delegate Anton Vos told the conference: "If Latin America is mentioned, why not name what is in the center of the world's attention at the moment, namely the invasion of Afghanistan? If we don't mention Afghanistan here, the WCC will be in danger of not being taken seriously."[10] Gunnar Staalsett of Norway said the Afghan people's right of self-determination had been violated, and that the WCC could not hide that fact and remain credible as an organization. His argument drew expressions of agreement from some Third World delegations, but the Russian delegations protested. The Russians claimed that the conference document would be devalued if an amend-ment concerning the Afghanistan situation were adopted.

Finally, conference delegates agreed that no countries would be identified specifically in the statement on "Human Struggles." The compromise document as adopted was both vague and weak.

The compromise did not, however, close the matter. Several other attempts were made to incorporate the issue of the Soviet invasion of Afghanistan into the conference proceedings. On the meeting's last day, for example, the Rev. Michael Nazir-Ali of Pakistan proposed that the conference condemn the Soviet military action and repression of human rights in Afghanistan. Nazir-Ali's proposal was immediately opposed by Russian Orthodox Archbishop Makary, who declared:

> The aim of this conference is to unite us. I think we must stick to this aim. Please understand the Russian Orthodox delegation. We represent millions of believers in the Soviet Union. Our people share the policy of our government, which purports to give the Afghan government the assistance it asked for.[11]

Another Russian delegate (not Russian Orthodox) went so far as to state that his church's "participation in the WCC would be subject to reconsideration" if the conference condemned the Soviet action in Afghanistan.

After another deadlock on the issue, the conference adopted a resolution which acknowledged that there were other international crises of concern to the WCC that were not addressed in the official pronouncements. This resolution stated:

> We wish to state that the mentioning of specific countries and situations in the resolutions of this conference is partly to be attributed to current events in those countries. We recognize, however, that there are other countries where foreign powers are intervening militarily, and governments which oppress, exploit, imprison, and kill innocent people. We may be able to identify some of those countries and peoples. Others, however, we dare not identify for the simple reason that such a public identification by the Conference may endanger the position—even the lives—of many of our brothers and sisters, some of whom are participating in this Conference.
>
> We therefore confess our inability to be as prophetic as we ought to be, as that may, in some instances, entail imposing martyrdom on our fellow believers in those countries—something we dare not

do from a safe distance. We know that many of them suffer under different regimes for their faith in Jesus Christ and urge that freedom of conscience be respected as well as other human rights. At the same time, we want to assure our unnamed brothers and sisters in many unnamed countries that we have not forgotten them; we identify strongly in their suffering for the kingdom of God.[12]

Central Committee compromises

The same debate occupied the WCC's Central Committee when it met in August 1980. The question was whether to endorse the Council's Executive Committee statement "Threats to Peace" which did in fact condemn the Soviet intervention.

The Rev. Johannes Langhoff of Denmark insisted that the committee endorse the "Threats to Peace" condemnation of the Soviet invasion. His proposal was quickly opposed by representatives of churches in the Eastern bloc. Other delegates expressed disappointment that the WCC was one-sided on the subject of human rights violations. The Rt. Rev. Per Loenning of Norway said the Council should express an "appeal of solidarity with the suffering people of Afghanistan as well as some words about Kampuchea." Loenning's latter reference was to the Southeast Asian country formerly known as Cambodia in which from one to three million people had been systematically slaughtered by the Pol Pot regime between 1975 to 1978. Loenning noted that the WCC had protested the Vietnam War during the 1960s and 1970s—and had been especially critical of U.S. policy in the war. He said it would therefore be inappropriate for the WCC not to speak with equal emphasis about the Soviet invasion of Afghanistan.[13]

During the ensuing debate, Russian Orthodox Archbishop Kirill said it had been difficult for him to agree to the "Threats to Peace" text approved by the Council's Executive Committee. Since that time, his position had become even more difficult, as he explained:

> This document was subsequently misused by Western media in such a way that in my situation special difficulties arose. Initially the paper was a basis for dialogue, but now the impression had been made that we had given in to political and inimical propaganda. Therefore, the paper became a point of division in my church, which created many difficulties.
>
> I do not doubt the validity of this paper, but I want to point to its consequences.[14]

In an interview, the Council's general secretary, Dr. Philip Potter, confirmed that the WCC Executive Committee's statement about "Threats to Peace" had, indeed, created problems for Russian Orthodox Church representatives to the worldwide organization:

> I think the point about the attitude of the Russians is simply this. When the statement of the Executive Committee was announced and it was known that it was a statement which was unanimously agreed upon, immediately various Western radio stations beamed to Russia stating that the WCC had spoken against the Afghanistan intervention and that the Russian representative (Kirill) had agreed. That was before they had the full statement in their hands. And, naturally, being placed in that situation, (the Russians) had to express themselves, that a very unfair way of reporting the statement of the WCC had put them in an extremely difficult position vis-à-vis their own state.[15]

Potter also pointed out that the WCC had not addressed events in Afghanistan in isolation, but had considered them in the context of international issues. Expressing the same sentiment was the Rev. Alexey Bichkov, a Russian Baptist, who said: "Some people condemn (the Soviet action in) Afghanistan, but it is my opinion that previous action may have created the events in Afghanistan."[16]

The Central Committee resolved the matter on 21 August 1980 by adopting a compromise statement that simply referred to the Executive Committee's "Threats to Peace" document. Consequently, the Central Committee did not adopt a separate statement or resolution condemning the Soviet invasion—as the Committee usually does in many other situations involving non-Communist states:

> The Central Committee, in the light of the statement "Threats to Peace" adopted by the Executive Committee of the WCC in Liebfrauenberg, France, in February 1980, expresses its deep continuing concern regarding prevailing threats to peace, including those mentioned in the statement, and urges that peaceful solutions be sought through negotiations involving the participation of all parties concerned and with all states observing the principles of sovereign equality, mutual security, territorial integrity, respect for the lawful interests of each party, and non-interference in the internal affairs of other countries.[17]

In his interview, Potter offered the following explanation for the large difference in tone between the WCC's "Threats to Peace" statement and its denunciation of North Korea's invasion of South Korea in 1950:

> In the first place we are dealing with quite different situations. Take, for example, Korea, where there was a strong Christian community, and a strong Western position in the (WCC) Central Committee which expressed itself. But in the case of Afghanistan, you have a situation where first of all there is no Christian community; the country involved is strongly pagan. So one cannot refer to it in the same way.
>
> The issue is not whether or not we spoke on Afghanistan—we did—but people only abstracted what already had been said by us about Afghanistan. The point is that what is happening in Afghanistan is related to many other events. It is related to the decisions made by NATO last December, to what is going on in the Middle East, the whole business of China, and all the rest. So we did not avoid mentioning Afghanistan, but we related Afghanistan to the many other issues that are threatening the peace of the world today.[18]

Whether knowingly or not, Potter's explanation generally reflected the Soviet Union's own position. According to the Soviets, the invasion was necessary to contain "threats to peace" in the region, including alleged attempts by China to destabilize the pro-Soviet Afghanistan government.

Only a few days after the Central Committee meeting of August 1980, the Christian Peace Conference (CPC) convened in Budapest. The CPC's president, Hungarian Bishop Karoly Toth, regularly attends WCC Central Committee meetings, and is also deeply involved in the pro-Soviet World Peace Council (WPC). Both the CPC and WPC are known front organizations of the International Department of the Communist party of the Soviet Union.[19] Present as an observer at the CPC consultation was Ninan Koshy, an official of the WCC's Commission on International Affairs (CCIA).

Like the WCC Executive Committee's "Threats to Peace" document, the CPC consultation concluded that the Soviet invasion of Afghanistan should be understood in the context of other international issues.[20] Earlier that year, the CPC had gone on record in defense of the Soviet invasion, suggesting that the Soviet Union was compelled to "honor the request" for help it had received from the government of Afghanistan.[21]

Equivocation at Vancouver, 1983

When the WCC's Sixth Assembly met in Vancouver, British Columbia, in August 1983, the Soviet invasion of Afghanistan was, of course, a dominant theme among many delegates. As the most representative of all WCC bodies, the Assembly could not ignore an issue of such importance to so many individuals and churches involved in the ecumenical movement. After extensive consultations with representatives of member churches from both East and West, the WCC's leadership agreed to draft a statement that essentially endorsed efforts by the United Nations' general secretary to find means for ending the conflict in Afghanistan.[22] Because the Soviet Union had already endorsed the United Nations' efforts, the draft text was acceptable to delegates of the Russian Orthodox church, and also to Eastern bloc churches which look to the Russians for guidance in ecumenical affairs. Moreover, many delegates from Western churches were relieved that the WCC was at last to address the Soviet invasion of Afghanistan.

The draft text proposed a peaceful resolution of the conflict in Afghanistan based upon "negotiations among the parties concerned (which) will lead to a comprehensive settlement." Such a settlement could be reached, the draft suggested, if several conditions were met:

1. an end to the supply of arms to the opposition groups from outside;
2. creation of a favorable climate for the return of the refugees;
3. a guarantee of the peace settlement by the Soviet Union, the United States, the People's Republic of China, and Pakistan;
4. withdrawal of Soviet troops from Afghanistan in the context of an overall political settlement, including an agreement between Afghanistan and the USSR.[23]

Russian Orthodox delegates called the draft statement "balanced and realistic," and made it clear that any other text would be unacceptable. Potter and staff members of the CCIA supported the Russian Orthodox position. No serious opposition was expected in the Assembly's Plenary Session because the draft proposal's four conditions were part of the proposals put forward by the United Nations general secretary.

Contrary to expectations, however, the draft generated considerable opposition when it was brought to the assembly floor on 9 August just before the meeting was to adjourn. Simon Prins of South Africa protested that, "We are really trying to avoid mentioning what is happening (in Afghanistan)."[24] Bishop Alexander Malik of the church of Pakistan proposed that the resolution be amended to call for "unconditional withdrawal of Soviet troops from Afghanistan." Malik charged that the drafting committee had "selected the weakest possible language. If it had been any Western country, the WCC would have jumped on it and denounced the country in the strongest possible language."[25]

Malik's proposal was rejected, but the debate continued. Other proposed amendments were ruled unacceptable by William P. Thompson, of the United Presbyterian Church, U.S.A., who was chairman of the drafting committee. Thompson said that the text as presented was "the least that could be accepted by one side, the most that could be accepted by the other." Bishop David Preus of the American Lutheran Church, U.S.A., then proposed that the assembly delete the requirement that outside countries stop supplying arms to Afghan resistance fighters. He also recommended that "immediate" withdrawal of Soviet troops be made the first priority of the WCC pronouncement.

Russian Orthodox delegates rejected Preus's proposals. Russian Orthodox Metropolitan Yuvenaliy said a call for unconditional withdrawal of Soviet troops from Afghanistan was simply not acceptable. The Soviets would withdraw their troops when conditions allowed them to do so, he said, but "immediate withdrawal at this moment is not feasible." Russian Orthodox Archbishop Kirill emphasized that "any changes in the text as accepted by the drafting committee would be politically misused. I therefore urge you to accept it in the efficiency of our joint effort." Otherwise, Kirill threatened, Russian churches' "Loyalty to the ecumenical movement would be challenged."[26]

The root of the matter for the Russian delegates was the draft text's call for outside groups to end their supply of arms to Afghan resistance fighters. Russian church delegates also approved of the resolution's endorsement of Soviet occupation until "an overall political settlement including agreement between Afghanistan and the USSR" could be reached. That provision meant in effect that the invader was authorized to set the terms of withdrawal.

Thompson defended the draft text by insisting that its four provisions were essentially a summary of proposals previously put forward by the U.N. general secretary. Thompson did not point out, however, that the United Nations General Assembly had called for the "immediate" withdrawal of foreign troops—Soviet troops—from Afghanistan. Many delegates incorrectly assumed that the WCC draft statement was identical to the United Nations position. This development prompted Bishop James Armstrong of the United Methodist Church, U.S.A., to tell the assembly,

"We vote in this body not as an extension of the United Nations, but as members of the World Council whose Lord is Jesus Christ."

The Preus-proposed amendment was then rejected on a vote of 306 to 278 with 35 abstentions. Subsequently, the resolution as drafted was approved on a vote of 479 to 21, with 142 abstentions.

As adopted, the resolution did not condemn the Soviet Union for invading Afghanistan. The WCC statement acknowledges only that "the continuing fighting there has led to tremendous suffering for vast sections of the population, many of whom have become refugees." Nor did the resolution define the Soviet invasion as the cause of the suffering in Afghanistan. Instead, it merely expresses the WCC's "concern regarding the Afghan situation expressed in earlier statements" by the WCC.[27]

In a later interview, the Rt. Rev. Arne Rudvin, Bishop of Karachi in Pakistan, who had gone to Pakistan from Norway as a missionary twenty-seven years earlier, expressed deep disappointment in the Vancouver resolution:

> I have great difficulty in respecting the World Council of Churches. It seems to me that it has fully compromised with the Russian Church and that it is bending over backwards not to offend the Russians.
>
> Imagine a World Council of Churches being similarly pressured by the so-called German Christians in the late thirties and the Second World War so that it could not condemn Hitler's actions in Europe. That would be a parallel to what the WCC has done in Vancouver. It has now been shown that the WCC is not truly representing the Church of Christ, but is a political body. I cannot have any respect for its attitude.[28]

In defending the WCC's action, Potter told a press conference on the assembly's last day that, "If there is one thing the WCC will never do, it is to try to dodge issues."[29]

Potter's successor, Emilio Castro, later characterized the Vancouver Assembly's debate on Afghanistan as "the best service that could be offered for the sad situation in that country." The 1988 Geneva agreements on Afghanistan, he felt, had vindicated the positions taken up by the WCC.[30]

But the Geneva Accords concerning Afghanistan had not been the result of the WCC's call for an end to military supplies to the resistance. On the contrary, what had really forced the Soviets into making concessions was the resilience of those who fought a war of liberation which the WCC never recognized as such. While other liberation movements got all the WCC's sympathy, Afghan liberation fighters were told by the Vancouver Assembly that badly needed military aid should be cut off.

Indeed, there would have been no agreement on Afghanistan if the Soviet attempt to isolate the resistance had been followed up. In failing to recognize the just cause of the resistance the WCC became subject to Soviet manipulation and even blackmail.

Central American Liberation Theology

The WCC, Liberation Theology and Nicaragua

Christian churches played an important role in organizing and sustaining the revolt of July 1979 which toppled the corrupt and oppressive regime of General Anastasio Somoza Debayle in Nicaragua. Many of the "revolutionary Christians" who joined the alliance of forces led by the Sandinista National Liberation Front (FSLN) viewed the strategic merger of religion and Marxism-Leninism as "a sign of hope for all of Latin America."[1] Nicaraguan Roman Catholic priests still participate in the Sandinista government, a pro-Cuban regime that embraces Marxist ideas. Their goal is to make Nicaragua a model for socially concerned Christians all over the world.[2]

Such activism on the part of the churches, fit neatly within the contours of what came to be known in the late 1960s as "liberation theology." Liberation theology invokes biblical concepts such as the "Kingdom of God," "Salvation," "Justice" and "Exodus" to justify revolutionary violence against a nonsocialist order allegedly based on repression of the people. Many liberation theologians seek "a radical change in the foundations of society, that is, the private ownership of the means of production,"[3] toward a socialist order. Liberation theologians generally regard the poor as Marx regarded the proletariat—as the source of a revolutionary political "liberation." Other Marxist concepts frequently appear in liberationist writings as well. "Class struggle" and "revolution" are usually accepted as means to overcome "structural violence."

Such an approach represents an attempt to politicize theological concepts or to theologize political (usually Marxist) concepts. Religion and revolution become intertwined to such a degree that Christian participation in revolutions, even violent ones, is virtually deemed obligatory. After all, the argument goes, if Christ and His Spirit are present and active in history, "every attempt to evade the struggle for a more just and more human world is the greatest infidelity to God."[4]

From its creation, this marriage of religion and revolutionary politics met with profound sympathy within the World Council of Churches. The Council had for years flirted with similar theological concepts regarding revolutionary movements in Africa and Latin America. Nicaragua was the latest revolutionary model in a line that included the originally much favored but now discredited Communist revolutions in Vietnam, Cambodia and Laos. A WCC team visiting Nicaragua shortly after the revolution reported that it was impressed by the spirit of the Nicaraguan people, and convinced "of the determination of the government to initiate immediate innovative programs of reconstruction."[5]

Faith in the Nicaraguan experiment was not shaken by the rapid social and political deterioration there over the following years. A prominent revolutionary leader, Edén Pastora, soon started accusing the Sandinistas of betraying the revolution. He was not the only one. Many who previously espoused the Sandinista cause were disillusioned with their actual policies. But their voices went unheeded. Instead, ecumenical leaders took heart when Brazilian educator Paulo Freire, who had previously been responsible for the WCC's "Education for Liberation" program, was asked to assist the Nicaraguan government in devising a literacy campaign. Freire embraces the total politicization of education: in his view, education must lead to revolution and after a revolution occurs should protect and sustain it.[6] Freire's literacy campaign was not popular education, but mass ideological indoctrination.

The director of the Permanent Commission for Human Rights (CPDH) in Managua, José Esteban González, was arrested in February 1981 on the grounds that he posed a threat to public security when all he had done, apparently, was protest the widespread practice of torture and the disappearance of political prisoners.[7] His arrest did not cause an outcry in ecumenical circles (as had, for example, the death on 14 March 1983 in El Salvador of a well-known human rights activist, Marianella Gracia Villas).[8] Nor did ecumenical circles respond to the Nicaraguan Commission of Jurists' report that 8,655 prisoners were killed in Sandinista prisons between 19 July 1979 and 31 December 1982.[9]

In May 1980, Gonzáles was told by the Rev. Charles R. Harper of the WCC's Human Rights Resources Office on Latin America that the Council would no longer support the commission financially. Harper's explanation was that the Council believed that human rights were now guaranteed by the Nicaraguan government.[10]

In September 1986 the author was informed by the present CPDH director, Lino Hernandez, that the WCC had not shown any interest in the Commission's work, even though political and civil liberties in Nicaragua had been increasingly curbed during the 1980-1986 period.

Indeed, even as freedom of the press was severely curbed, prisoners tortured, Indian minorities robbed of land rights, populations of whole villages "relocated," and churches in the Atlantic Coast area (where most of these minorities had lived for centuries) burnt, the 1983 WCC Assembly in Vancouver pronounced the achievements of the Nicaraguan people "life-affirming" and "commended" the Nicaraguan Christian community for its active participation in the building of national institutions and reconciliatory processes leading to peace with justice.[11]

The people's church
After enjoying the support of many Christians in the struggle against Somoza, the Sandinistas attempted to control the Catholic community in Nicaragua through the formation of a "popular" or "people's" church which they contrasted with the traditional hierarchical or "reactionary" church. That the Sandinistas' initiative threatened a serious break with traditional church doctrine and authority was obvious to the Nicaraguan bishops. These developments also worried Pope John Paul II, who in August 1982 issued a message that accused the so-called popular church of yielding to political ideologies and sowing discord. As Archbishop Miguel Obando y Bravo declared of the Sandinista revolution in June 1981: "After two years of hope, our revolution is drifting toward Marxism according to the Cuban model."[12] Obviously, the archbishop was afraid that this tendency would have serious implications for the church.

But the WCC continued to sympathize with the popular church. For example, although a priest in Baco was arrested by government security forces when he read the pope's message in his own church,[13] and although several Moravian church ministers were arrested for protesting the government's treatment of Indians, a WCC team found in Nicaragua:

...no recognizable "persecution" of the church. Three Catholic priests are ministers of government; a score of others work in various levels of government. Four Sandinista commandantes, we were told, had recently had their children baptized. The Institute of Nicaraguan Cinema, under the Ministry of Culture, has produced a film called *Gracias a Dios y la Revolucion* about Christian participation in the revolution. Radio time is given on the Sandinista station for church programs on Sundays.[14]

Three years later, ten Catholic priests were expelled from Nicaragua for alleged "anti-government activity." The expulsions followed a march by more than 300 people, five of the ten priests among them, led by Archbishop Miguel Obando y Bravo of Managua, in support of Father Amana Pena, a priest accused of aiding anti-Sandinista rebels. According to the archbishop, the expulsion was "the answer from the Interior Ministry to our march. This is evidence that Marxism is trying to eliminate the church in Nicaragua because Marxism is the enemy of the Church."[15]

Amnesty International later investigated the incident and found that the Nicaraguan State Security Service (DGSE) had fabricated evidence against Father Pena. The DGSE had produced a film purporting to show Father Pena leaving a car holding a bag which, when opened, revealed a "terrorist kit." The film was used to imply that the Catholic church was involved in armed opposition to the government. Father Pena claimed that the bag was given him by a security service member who had asked him to deliver it to another person. Indeed, the DGSE made a video recording of Father Pena presenting the bag to another individual, after which he was placed under house arrest. Amnesty International considered Father Pena a prisoner of conscience falsely implicated in criminal activity by the state security service because of his political views.[16]

The WCC Central Committee meeting in Geneva at the time ignored Father Pena's arrest. The Rev. Emilio Castro of Uruguay, newly-appointed WCC general secretary, refused to pass judgement on the incident, and said in an interview that "it is totally unfair to talk about clamping down on religious freedom in Nicaragua."[17] It is fair to ask, however, what the general secretary's reaction would have been had a similar incident occurred in, say, El Salvador or the Philippines.

Repression of Indian minorities

The Sandinista regime's repressive character was most apparent in its treatment of ethnic minorities, especially the Indians who live along the Atlantic

Coast. Most of the Indians are Moravian Christians who are attached both to their beliefs and their ancestral lands. Because they had been ill-treated by Somoza, many Indians initially sympathized with the Sandinistas.

By late 1979, however, the Sandinistas planned to integrate the indigenous peoples of the Atlantic Coast into the "revolutionary process." Professor Bernard Nietschmann of the University of California, Berkeley, who has closely observed events in Nicaragua, testified before the Inter-American Commission on Human Rights of the Organization of American States (OAS) that:

> The occurrence of arbitrary killings of Miskito civilians appears to be widespread. A pattern is readily seen. Miskito men and women are accused of being contras, tortured or threatened with death unless they confess, killed, and then reported as having been contras, if, indeed, there is any report at all.[18]

In another document, Nietschmann refers to "a policy of Indian genocide that is generated internally from the Sandinistas' own Marxist ideology and racist attitudes that deny the Indians the right to remain Indians."[19]

When the Indians resisted these persecutions, the FSLN responded with an escalating program of counterinsurgency. Professor Nietschmann believed that one-fourth of the 165,000 Indians were either in "relocation" or refugee camps; one-half of Miskito and Sumo villages had been destroyed; 1,000 Indian civilians were in prison, missing or dead; and Indian rights to self-government, land and resources had been abolished.[20]

The Sandinistas insisted that relocation of the Indians was unavoidable because of growing resistance activities in the border area where most of the Indians lived. But the relocation began well before any guerilla activity arose in the Atlantic Coast region. Indeed, much of the resistance was prompted by the Sandinistas' efforts to relocate the Indians.

When the WCC finally reacted to Sandinista atrocities against the Indians, it adopted the Sandinistas' version of events. The WCC Vancouver Assembly, for example, was quick to accept Sandinista explanation that the policy vis-á-vis the Indians was under review:

> The government [of Nicaragua] had demonstrated its openness in acknowledging the inappropriateness of some policies related to the Miskito Indian and other ethnic groups of the Atlantic Coast, and is moving towards reconciliation. It is also important to note that

the Nicaraguan process has involved the full participation of Christians, both Roman Catholic and Protestant, at every level of reconstruction and nation-building.[21]

And in investigating the charges against the Sandinistas, the WCC seemed to do little more than acknowledge that some abuses had occurred. A "Progess Report" on Miskito Indians, published by the WCC's Commission of Inter-Church Aid, Refugee and World Service (CICARWS) recognized only that there had been some abuses, and suggested that the Indians should be willing to cooperate with the government as much as possible.[22] WCC staff also reacted positively when a few pro-Sandinista Miskitos formed their own organization in July 1984.

This stance differs greatly from the WCC's defense of Indians in other lands. For example, a WCC booklet on Land Rights for Indigenous People published by the WCC's Program to Combat Racism (PCR), deals with the case histories of minority treatment in Australia, Brazil and Canada. The publication makes no reference to the Indian minorities in Nicaragua.[23] In June 1982, the WCC's Central Committee adopted a statement on "Land Rights for Indigenous People" which conspicuously excluded the Nicaraguan case:

The denial of political power has allowed treaties to be abrogated (Canada, USA, New Zealand); land to be expropriated (Mexico, Puerto Rico, Guatemala); people to be forcibly relocated (Brazil, Paraguay, Philippines); and policies of assimilation to be implemented (Chile, Australia, Colombia).[24]

Put quite simply, the WCC had come to treat abuses of human rights in Nicaragua in the same manner as it regards—or disregards—those committed by Eastern bloc governments. When the WCC's own Ecumenical Press Service (EPS) reported a protest by the Roman Catholic bishops of Nicaragua against the Sandinistas' resettlement of about 8,500 Miskito Indians, great pains were taken to present the official Sandinista explanation:

[The government] called the church protest political, coinciding with similar complaints from the U.S. government and designed to damage national unity. It said the Indians are better off away from the Nicaragua-Honduras border, where there have been military clashes in recent weeks. Earlier in February, the government said it uncovered a plot to promote an uprising in the Miskito area. It said the effort involved non-Nicaraguan army officers, an opposition leader, and some church workers in the area. Some clergy have been detained in connection with these similar activities.[25]

The WCC wanted to support, not criticize, the Nicaraguan revolution—at least that is what Miskito spokesman Silvio Diaz was told when in March 1984 he took his case to staff members of the WCC Program to Combat Racism (PCR) and the CCIA. Since the Council basically sympathized with the Sandinistas, a PCR staff member told Diaz, it could intervene on behalf of the Indians only by quiet diplomacy.[26] Hence the Vancouver Assembly's "Statement on Central America" merely "affirms and encourages the process of reconciliation among Nicaraguan minorities and the Spanish-speaking majority and urges the Nicaraguan government to maintain its openness and commitment to increasing the sensitivity of its policy and practice in this area."[27]

The WCC's generous understanding

A WCC delegation visiting Nicaragua in September 1983 was "impressed by the statesmanlike attitudes of both Moravian church leaders and government leaders as all seek to heal a painful and difficult relationship."[28]

The delegation acknowledged that the policy of relocating the Indians had caused a great deal of resentment, and that Indian leaders and pastors who protested the policy had been jailed and accused of opposing the revolution. "However," the delegation added, "the leadership of the Church supports the revolutionary process and insists that official actions taken against its institutions and employees are not a case of religious persecution."[29]

In denying that the Sandinistas' goal is "to establish a totalitarian Marxist state," the delegation said it was impressed by "the pluralism in the government, the service of Christians, lay and clergy at every level of government."

The delegation's report also reflected a remarkable perspective on press censorship:

Though we are supporters of a free press, we can understand some of the particularities of Nicaragua that argue for the present press censorship.[30]

The Sandinistas' actions were therefore to be excused because their government was deemed "a sign and transmitter of hope."[31]

On the basis of this favorable evaluation, the WCC delegation recommended:

> In the light of the pervasive and clear participation of Christians in the past and present defense of liberation in Nicaragua, churches worldwide are invited to learn from the unique experiment being lived by their Nicaraguan sisters and brothers in the Christian communities. Particular attention should be given to the spirituality of struggle, the ecumenical cooperation at community levels and the fresh articulation of the theological and biblical roots of Christian participation in the transformation of society. Churches and Christians are urged to visit Nicaragua and to share their insights and experiences with their parishes and congregations worldwide.[32]

In July 1985 another WCC delegation visited Nicaragua, and also Honduras, Guatemala and El Salvador. It consisted of Charles R. Harper, William P. Thompson, who was a member of the WCC Central Committee; and two WCC presidents, Dr. Marga Buehrig, Switzerland, and Metropolitan Paulos Mar Gregorios from India. The dominant figure within that delegation was Gregorios, one of the most influential of the WCC presidents and also deeply involved in two Soviet Communist party fronts: the Christian Peace Conference in Prague and the World Peace Council (WPC) in Helsinki.

In view of this it was only logical that the WCC delegation, while in Nicaragua, only contacted government and progovernment groups, and paid a "solidarity visit" to the Nicaraguan foreign minister, Miguel d'Escoto who was on a hunger strike to protest U.S. policy in Central America. The delegates also talked with Nicaraguan President Daniel Ortega. Ortega assured the WCC officials that "Sandinism" is based on "the Christian principles of our Christian people."[33]

The delegation reported on its travels to the subsequent WCC Central Committee meeting in Buenos Aires. There, Metropolitan Gregorios informed a press conference that "Christians in Nicaragua see their government not as Marxist-inspired."[34] Other delegation members echoed that belief, although they admitted that the delegation had not paid attention to groups inside Nicaragua that oppose the Sandinistas. For example, the delegation did not even contact the Managua-based "Permanent Commission on Human Rights" (CPDH), which takes a line independent of the government, or the Roman Catholic hierarchy led by Cardinal Miguel Obando y Bravo, who had been a critic of the Somoza dictatorship and later became a critic of the Sandinistas.[35] However, when in El Salvador, the delegation did attempt to meet members of the Roman Catholic hierarchy.

While in Nicaragua, the delegation endorsed "liberation theology." This was made clear during a visit to the Ecumenical Institute of Antonio Valdivieso in Managua. This institute is one of the most important centers of liberation theology in Central America.

The endorsement was also reflected in a "pastoral letter" which the WCC's Central Committee in Buenos Aires adopted after hearing the delegation's report. The letter expressed the WCC's sympathy with the Sandinista position, and noted that "everywhere (in Central America) the actions of the United States were observed."

The letter further stated that the U.S. was involved "in support for the present government in El Salvador; in promoting militarization of Costa Rica and Honduras; in economic and diplomatic measures as well as constantly increasing military threats against Nicaragua."[36] Never has the WCC spoken with such clarity on Soviet activities in, for example, Afghanistan.

WCC statements on Central America cannot be seen in isolation from deliberate Soviet and Cuban propaganda efforts on behalf of left wing forces in that region. Occasionally, the WCC does not even hesitate to cooperate with notorious Soviet Communist party front organizations to have U.S. policies condemned. Thus, the WCC's Commission on International Affairs (CCIA) and the Soviet controlled World Peace Council (WPC) were among the organizations to prepare an "International Conference on Nicaragua and for Peace in Central America," held in Lisbon, 3-6 May 1984.[37] This event was basically Communist inspired. Portuguese Prime Minister Mario Soares, a Social Democrat, discouraged his friends in the Socialist International from attending.

The WCC's tendency to rebuke the United States while more or less exonerating pro-Soviet or Marxist regimes was noted with approval in Eastern Europe. The East German communist newspaper *Neues Deutschland* praised the WCC for "chastising U.S. policy in Central America."[38]

El Salvador

By 1982, when 70 percent of El Salvador's electorate went to the polls despite a massive guerrilla campaign of disruption and intimidation, U.S. policy toward El Salvador could tentatively be judged a success. By 1984, when José Napoleon Duarte won the presidency in free and fair elections, the situation looked even better. The United States had always justified its controversial aid for the previous military regime in El Salvador as an essential component of an evolutionary process toward a parliamentary democracy. The United States saw the Salvadoran elections of 1982 and 1984 as far more valuable to El Salvador's future than any violent revolution would have been. Many Salvadorans agreed. The Catholic bishops of El Salvador, in a statement made with the approval of the Vatican, deemed the first round of elections "a peaceful way for the majority of the people who have said 'no' to violence to have the opportunity to express their will."[39]

The WCC, however, was of a different mind concerning El Salvador. The Council did not share the bishop's sentiments, nor did it support the country's 1984 elections. Indeed, at the 1983 Vancouver Assembly, the WCC made a point of not including the Salvadoran 1982 elections among what it termed the "promising signs of life" in Latin America. Instead, the WCC at its Vancouver Assembly chose to celebrate the "forces of historic change" in El Salvador.[40] And what were these forces? They were those forces in the region most imperiled by American influence. The WCC unequivocally opposed U.S. policy in the region which, it said, "is publicly articulated as a framework within which the objectives of peace, reform, economic development and democracy can be achieved and communism and 'export of revolution' prevented."[41]

The WCC discounted the stability attributable at least in part to U.S. policies toward El Salvador, and the American pressures which helped bring about the 1982 elections.

The 1983 WCC statement went on to urge "the government of El Salvador to enter into a fruitful process of dialogue with representatives of its political and military opposition, so as to bring longlasting peace to the country."[42] It did not seem to matter to the WCC that the Salvadoran guerrillas had seen their popular support dwindle dramatically as the process of democratic and economic reforms proved to be successful. The Marxist guerrillas claimed that "the Christian Democratic Party (led by Duarte) does not have the least amount of popular support."[43] Subsequent elections, boycotted by the guerillas who oppose parliamentary democracy, proved their predictions to be entirely wrong. The guerrillas' failed call for a general uprising, a "final offensive," in January 1981, was also ignored. For many in the WCC, however, the only real political and military opposition in El Salvador was to be found in the camp of the guerrillas.

It is quite unlikely that anyone in the WCC had the slightest sympathy for the extreme right-wing "ARENA" party which was an important opposition to Duarte. The WCC seemed to think that a real solution to the difficulties in El Salvador could not be found in elections but in the government dealing directly with the guerrillas. CCIA Director Ninan Koshy said that the most promising result of Duarte's election was that "prospects for negotiations with the opposition" were therefore improved.[44] At other times, the WCC has less obliquely expressed its impatience with strictly parliamentary solutions to Central American problems. In 1980, for example, the WCC Central Committee drew special attention to a National Council of Churches' (NCC) resolution calling for the United States to "grasp the historic moment and update and transform its traditional policy in Central America by seeking to respond positively to popular forces emerging in El Salvador."[45] For the WCC, the guerrillas were the "popular forces" whose cause the liberation theologians so heartily espoused.

By comparison, the WCC's Vancouver Assembly criticized the Salvadoran government for having "demonstrated an inability to curb human rights violations and implement needed reform."[46] Indeed, on balance, the Vancouver Assembly saw only the negative aspects of U.S. involvement in Central America. That the United States could—and actually did—press for reform and democratic structures was completely ignored, not only by the Vancouver Assembly, but by almost every statement on Central America issued by the WCC.

A double standard

The WCC's indifference to, and near hostility toward, the first stirrings of parliamentary democracy in El Salvador was consistent with the Council's conviction that no good could come of U.S. attempts to replace totalitarian rule in Central America with democratic governments. Of course, U.S. policy toward Central America has not been perfect either in conception or execution. The U.S. made major mistakes in mining the territorial waters of Nicaragua. The overall U.S. policy toward Central America, however, was based upon a desire to promote democracy and human rights in a region vital to U.S. interests. The WCC laid all emphasis on U.S. military presence and activities. Consequently, the WCC's response to a wave of violence sponsored by so-called "death squads" in El Salvador in the late 1970s and early 1980s was fairly predictable. The WCC World Conference on Mission and Evangelism in Melbourne in May 1980 issued a lengthy "Declaration on El Salvador" that condemned "the support of the military intervention of the United States of America." The Conference recommended "that a letter be sent to the President of the United States of America appealing to his government to stop support and military aid to military regimes, and to respect the right of the people of Latin America to seek a new social order that is more just and more humane."[47] On a number of occasions over the next few years, the WCC made its animus toward the United States even more explicit. In a 1981 letter to the newly-formed Latin American Council of Churches, for example, WCC General Secretary Philip Potter blamed the United States' administration for social and political problems in Central America: "It claims an improvement in the human rights situation in order to continue military and economic assistance," Potter said of U.S. policy.[48] At the WCC Central Committee's meeting in Dresden later that year, the United States was asked "to desist from all direct or covert, present or planned intervention in the countries of Central America and the Caribbean."[49]

Occasionally, as with the Vancouver Assembly's statement that the Council "vigorously opposes any type of military intervention by the United States, covert or overt, or by any other government in the Central American region,"[50] there was some hint that the WCC recognized that the United States has not been the only country involved in Central American issues. However, by refusing to identify other involved governments, the WCC effectively ignored Cuban and Soviet involvement in the region.

Some WCC staff members tended to dismiss indications that the Soviet Union supported guerrilla movements in Central America. For example, a 1981 report issued by two WCC staff members who had visited the region concluded:

> In spite of the repeated and virulent accusations on the part of the Reagan Administration, the role of the Soviet Union in the area has been surprisingly low-key, apart from its intensive relationship with Cuba. In the long term, the success of more pluralistic models, such as is being developed in Nicaragua, may even serve to more effectively limit the influence of the Soviet Union in the area.[51]

But the facts do not entirely support such a view. "Photographs don't lie," said U.S. Secretary of State Alexander Haig when he confronted Soviet Ambassador Anatoly Dobrynin with evidence documenting transhipment of Soviet arms through Nicaragua to insurgents in El Salvador.[52]

While the Christian Democrats and the new military high command were launching the reforms, Cuba and several other Communist countries were beginning a concerted effort to impose a Marxist-Leninist dictatorship by force. In meetings in Havana in December 1979 and May 1980, Fidel Castro helped FPL, ERP, and FARN to unite with the Moscow-line Salvadoran Communists into a guerrilla alliance...

Creating a unified military command and supplying modern armaments were only part of a broad political-military strategy. This strategy included training and an ideologically commited military cadre in Cuba and developing a concerted international propaganda campaign to discredit nonviolent solutions. Only the external elements of this Cuban strategy proved successful. Those elements that depended upon conditions inside El Salvador failed.[53]

Having achieved a united command over the extreme left, Salvadoran guerrilla leaders met in the Hungarian Embassy in Mexico City with representatives of Cuba, the USSR, Bulgaria, East Germany, Poland and Vietnam. In June and July of 1980, Salvadoran Communist leaders went to Moscow and then, with Soviet endorsement, visited East Germany, Bulgaria, Vietnam and Ethiopia. All of these countries promised military and other support. The Cuban-Soviet bloc military supply operation used Western weapons (some from Vietnam) as a "cover," and secretly shipped some 200 tons of weapons through Cuba and Nicaragua to arm Salvadoran guerrillas for their intense but unsuccessful "final offensive" in January 1981.[54]

In August 1986 the author interviewed two former Nicaraguan customs officials who confirmed that the Nicaraguan government at the highest level had been deeply involved in the smuggling of arms to El Salvador. They claimed that Managua gave them special orders to cooperate in the arms smuggling.[55]

Salvadoran guerrillas are trained both in Cuba and Nicaragua. As early as 1981 it was reported that there were at least thirteen guerrilla-training bases in Nicaragua. These camps were said to be in northwest Nicaragua, enabling insurgents to cross through Honduras into El Salvador.[56]

When in 1983 a delegation of U.S. Congressmen paid a visit to Nicaragua, the Sandinista government could not deny that it maintained a command and control center for the Salvadoran guerrillas in Managua.[57] Under the circumstances, Nicaraguan complaints of American intervention in Central America seem rather hypocritical.

Why does the WCC persist in downplaying Eastern bloc influence in Latin America? Part of the answer is that the Soviet Union's Western Hemisphere proxy, Cuba, is a favorite of both the WCC and the Conference of Caribbean Churches (CCC). The Council's CCIA, for example, considers it urgent that "normal diplomatic relations between the United States and Cuba be reestablished, the (U.S. trade) embargo ended, and trade established" between the two countries.[58] It is difficult to find even one public statement by the WCC on the subject of human rights violations in Cuba. Cuba is hardly ever targeted for any criticism by the WCC. This fact applies both to Cuba's domestic and foreign policies, including Cuba's extensive military operations in Africa.

The pro-Cuban lobby operates through such bodies as the Evangelical Council of Churches of Cuba (CIEC), the Cuban Resource Center, and the Conference for Caribbean Churches (CCC). These organizations discount as "exaggerated" reports of human rights violations in Cuba—even those documented by Amnesty International.[59] WCC staff members who visit Cuba sometimes return enthusiastic about Cuban society. A member of the WCC's Commission on the Churches' Participation in Development (CCPD) expressed admiration for the "Cuban experience":

> Our group is struggling to find some categories by which to judge the "Cuban experience" and wondering how to communicate this back to our countries and our churches. I notice that all of us when talking seem to imply that Cuban society shows a lot more signs of the Kingdom of God than many other societies we know of. How do we deal with this?[60]

While this opinion may not be shared by the WCC itself, it is true nonetheless that these "fellow travelers" and "political pilgrims" often have greater influence on official WCC statements than do those who hold contrary views. And in Central America, Cuban "signs of the Kingdom of God" have evidently become a model for the policies of the World Council of Churches.

Southern Africa
and the WCC's
"Program to Combat Racism"

A political or moral crusade?

One of the WCC's most praiseworthy aims finds expression in its worldwide "Program to Combat Racism" (PCR). Given the shameful record of some churches on racism, the WCC rightly seeks to rectify an evil that has caused so much suffering. Racism has manifested itself particularly in South Africa where the white minority government has suppressed legitimate demands since the accession of the Nationalist party to power in 1948 and the institution of apartheid with spurious legal forms. The WCC is perfectly right in focusing on this major problem.

But questions can be raised about how the WCC has conducted this crusade, and about why its efforts are largely political rather than moral. For example, the Council's World Consultation on "Racism in the 1980s," held in Noordwijkerhout, Holland, denounced "naïve assumptions such as the one that racism is a phenomenon which can be isolated from capitalism and imperialism." The Consultation went so far as to declare that "the international capitalist economic system" provides the foundation of "much of the racism experienced by people in the world today":

> The dominant economic system of the world is one ordered to promote the self-interest, greed, and values of the "white" world. This system exploits the natural and human resources of Third World peoples reducing them in the process to the status of impersonal units.[1]

This view entails many significant consequences. Insofar as this is a common view in the WCC—a strong likelihood since the Central Committee hailed the reports and commended them to member churches—it has meant that the WCC's war on racism has been far narrower in scope than it could have been. For example, the WCC has found it awkward to address injustices not directly related to capitalism—such as the treatment of Soviet Jews. (When asked about the PCR's silence on the subject of Soviet Jewry, the Noordwijkerhout Consultation's moderator, Wilfred Wood, lamely explained that "not every issue comes within [the PCR's] purview. It is not essentially a PCR matter.")[2]

The PCR has emphasized instead what Baldwin Sjollema, its former director, called "white institutional racism."[3] By that, Sjollema means that the WCC primarily focuses on racism in southern Africa. The WCC defined its position at the 1979 Central Committee meeting in Jamaica:

> The racism of *white peoples* was the most dangerous and powerful phenomenon that needed to be combatted more urgently than any other form of racism or ethnocentrism. By implication concentration on Southern Africa became mandatory.[4]

While this politicized approach has narrowed the WCC's perspective on racism, it has strengthened the Council's belief that racial injustice is the product of capitalistic economic systems. As a corollary, the Council has developed a new doctrine for combatting racism—by the violent overthrow of the political or social institutions held responsible for racist practices.

The PCR and "liberation movements" in Southern Africa

In 1983, the WCC's "Special Fund to Combat Racism" gave $70,000 to the African National Congress (ANC) and $105,000 to the South-West African People's Organization (SWAPO). Both of these groups espouse violent revolution. SWAPO also has authoritarian aims—as its leader, Sam Nujoma, admitted in a 1978 interview. "We fought the struggle. We alone are entitled to power, and we will not share it with anyone."[5] SWAPO also has close ties to the Soviet Union. Nujoma addressed the 1981 Soviet Communist Party Congress and praised the Party's general secretary, Leonid Brezhnev, as a champion of world peace, détente, freedom and human dignity.

The ANC also has close ties to the Soviet Union. Although not Communist in origin, the ANC has been infiltrated by elements linked to the pro-Soviet South African Communist Party (SACP). Today, these links are clear, and ANC leader Oliver Tambo has stated that the SACP is the ANC's natural ally. Furthermore, Tambo has consistently supported Soviet bloc initiatives. Under his leadership, the ANC has established close ties with other organizations committed to violence, including the Polisario Front, Fretelin and the Palestine Liberation Organization (PLO).[6]

For a long time both the ANC and SWAPO have been major recipients of WCC grants. But even more controversial was a 1978 decision to give $85,000 to Zimbabwe's "Patriotic Front." The Patriotic Front was one of a number of parties struggling for power in what was formerly called Rhodesia. It had been formed with the explicit purpose of countering the influence of the United African National Congress (UANC) led by Bishop Abel Muzorewa. In contravention of the WCC's claim not to identify with any political party or group, the $85,000 grant was widely interpreted as "a token of solidarity" with the forces of Patriotic Front leaders Robert Mugabe and Joshua Nkomo.[7] Front leaders themselves described the grant as an "endorsement by the WCC of its armed struggle."[8] The WCC suggested that other organizations seeking liberation for blacks in Zimbabwe were not as committed to the elimination of racism as the Patriotic Front.

The grant to the Patriotic Front was not the first time that the WCC had taken clear sides in the conflict between the races in Rhodesia— now known as Zimbabwe. But this grant was especially controversial because it was the culmination of a series of acts by which the WCC had seemingly exonerated the Patriotic Front of its alleged involvement in the murders of innocent people. For example, when guerrilla forces killed seven Roman Catholic missionaries in February of 1977, the WCC tended to lay the blame on the Rhodesian government, and suggested that:

> The atrocities perpetrated by all sides are clearly the result of the regime's persistent refusal to negotiate a peaceful settlement with the Zimbabwe leaders.[9]

The WCC deplored the killings, but declined to hold the guerrilla forces directly responsible.

The WCC was also unwilling to admit that Mugabe's ZANU guerrillas were responsible for a June 1978 attack on a Pentecostal missionary post at Elim near the Mozambique border. In that attack, three men, four women and four children died.[10] The Council accepted Mugabe's claim that the attack had been the work of the Rhodesian government's special anti-terrorist units—so-called "Selous Scouts"—pretending to be in ZANU ranks. Indeed, the WCC claimed to have "reports of at least one unit of the Rhodesian army...disguising themselves as freedom fighters and committing atrocities that are blamed on the liberation movements."[11] The main source of this information was the International Association of Democratic Lawyers, a known front organization of the Soviet Communist party. There was, however, no conclusive proof that the Elim massacre was the work of the Selous Scouts, and the army defector who claimed this was referring to incorrect information.[12] If anything, available evidence pointed to ZANU responsibility. In late August, when Rhodesian forces killed two ZANU fighters, one of them carried what appeared to be a diary in which the Elim massacre was described in great detail, suggesting that he had been involved in the killings.[13] Further, the area where the killings occurred is near an area where ZANU guerrillas operated.

WCC sympathies became even more apparent in September 1978 when guerrillas shot down an Air Rhodesia Viscount, resulting in the death of thirty-eight of the plane's fifty-six civilian passengers. According to a *Newsweek* account:

> One group of survivors was confronted by a handful of black anti-government guerrillas who suddenly emerged from the bush. "Please don't kill us," pleaded one of the whites. A guerrilla replied: "You have taken our land." The blacks opened fire with their Soviet-made Kalashnikov rifles. The next day, when Rhodesian paratroops dropped into the area, they found ten bodies, including those of seven women and two young girls, scattered across the bloodsodden field.[14]

The WCC reacted as it had to previous atrocities in the region. A spokesman said the Council "deeply deplores the reported shooting down of a civilian aircraft in Rhodesia," but he declined to identify those responsible.[15] Early in November 1978, PCR Director Sjollema told the Dutch press that the plane had been shot down by Nkomo's commanders but without Nkomo's approval. In fact, Nkomo had personally claimed responsibility for the act in an earlier interview.[16] It is difficult to believe that the Council would have hesitated to identify those responsible, and to condemn them, if such an atrocity had been committed by a group or government not supported by the WCC.

No doubt, the former Rhodesian armed forces also occasionally committed atrocities. But for some reason or another these seemed to get more attention from the WCC than those committed by the guerrillas.

Grant-generated controversy

The WCC's biased approach to the Rhodesian problem provoked severe criticism from its member churches. In the crisis that ensued—somewhat typically dismissed as "polarization" by some WCC staff members—the Salvation Army and the Presbyterian Church of Ireland suspended their WCC membership. In 1979 the Presbyterian Church of Ireland went further and formally withdrew from the WCC.

Irish churches—in a land torn by terrorist activities by both Protestant and Catholic radicals—argued that grants to groups such as the Patriotic Front would be interpreted as a WCC endorsement of terrorist violence. "We in Ireland feel that violence is undesirable," said Irish Anglican Canon Elliot at the WCC's Central Committee meeting in Jamaica. "The WCC is in danger of making the same mistake we made in Ireland when we identified ourselves with one political movement."[17]

Similar reactions came when the Norwegian Missionary Society put pressure on the Church of Norway to resign from the WCC. The Church of Norway resisted this pressure but criticism of WCC policies within this church mounted. Swiss churches, too, complained that political motives were being imposed on the WCC member churches.[18] The Evangelical Church of Germany (EKD) requested an investigation of the Special Fund from which WCC grants to so-called liberation movements are made.[19]

Much of the controversy came to a head at the Central Committee meeting in Jamaica. There, the Salvation Army's representative, Commissioner Harry Williams, proposed that grants from the WCC's "Special Fund to Combat Racism" be linked to the activities of local churches. His proposal, which was supported by David Russell of the Baptist Union of Great Britain and Ireland, recommended that, in awarding grants from the special fund, "use should be made wherever possible of indigenous church agencies to deliver the humanitarian services desired."[20]

The intent of the proposal was clear. If adopted, it would significantly limit the discretion of WCC bodies such as the Executive Committee to make grants to groups and movements on solely political bases. The resolution would shift grant-giving power to local churches whose influence in such matters had heretofore been minimal.

Understandably, WCC General Secretary Philip Potter opposed the proposal. He said the Russell-Williams proposal would "strike at a basic purpose of the grants from the Special Fund, namely, to express the WCC's solidarity with those struggling for freedom and justice."[21]

Potter was prepared to make some cosmetic concessions; instead of facing the problem, he defused the opposition. Potter persuaded Williams and Russell to withdraw their proposal by repeating a promise that the Special Fund and its grant criteria would be subject to a "process of consultations" with WCC member churches. He also assured them that the Russell-Williams proposal's criticism would be considered. In the end, however, the WCC Central Committee announced that administration of the Special Fund "has so far been in accordance with the established and accepted criteria set by the Central Committee and that the PCR should be encouraged to continue its work."[22]

Potter's success on this issue was short-lived. He was not able to appease all groups disgruntled by the grants to the Patriotic Front. Because of its radically anti-Western bias, the 1980 Consultation on "Racism in the 1980s" deepened the rift in the WCC over the Council's engagement in revolutionary politics. This in turn led to an even more serious blow: on 31 July 1981, after a fruitless talk with WCC leaders in Geneva, the Salvation Army—the world's largest nongovernmental social welfare organization, and a founding WCC member—informed the Council that it would withdraw its full membership and retain ony fraternal status. Although this was not a complete break with the WCC, the Salvation Army's decision highlighted the Council's politicization. The Salvation Army simply no longer wished to be party to it:

Our gravamen has to do with the issuance by the World Council of Churches of statements, the developing of policies and the carrying out of actions which we regard as political, and which, as such endanger the non-political nature of the Army, the preservation of which is basic to the Movement's effectiveness in a number of countries. Refusal to identify with political factions, as distinct from deep social concern for the needy people of all lands regardless of creed, color, or political persuasion, has been the essence of the Army's life and endeavour from its very beginning. Indeed, we see clearly that any such political identification would inevitably cut us off from large numbers of those very people we seek to succour. The Salvation Army's foundation belief is that the only real hope for the transformation of society lies in personal salvation through faith in the redemptive grace of Christ.[23]

The WCC Central Committee received this news of the Salvation Army's decision "with deep regret." In reply, however, the committee expressed its disagreement with the distinction drawn by the Salvation Army "between the so-called political nature of the action of the WCC and the claim of the Salvation Army to have a non-political stance."[24]

The dispute took several concrete forms. For example, much of the WCC's criticism of the South African government was certainly justified. But the Salvation Army correctly pointed out that revolutionary violence is not likely to solve the problems of southern Africa. Like many churches committed to justice in South Africa, the Salvation Army argued that revolutionary violence in South Africa would only provoke much more violence, and result in massive new bloodshed instead of peaceful resolutions to longstanding difficulties. The Salvation Army had a good historical case; the many violent revolutions in the twentieth century have rarely resulted in improved social, economic and political conditions. Indeed, it would be easier to argue the contrary.

In a lengthy "Statement on Southern Africa," the WCC's 1983 Vancouver Assembly pointed out that "institutionalized racism in South Africa continues to be the central problem of justice and peace in the region." Any theological justification of apartheid, by the South African government, or by churches, the statement deemed "a heretical perversion of the Gospel."[25] The Vancouver Assembly also condemned the "Bantustan policy" of "nominally independent tribal homelands."

The Vancouver statement referred to South African government proposals to grant "colored" ministers and Asians a limited representation in a multicameral legislature as "inherently racist." Such proposals, the statement continued, "emphasize separation between the races rather than integration, and underscore the fact that blacks continue to be excluded entirely from the political process."[26] Although this was quite true, it was not evident that the WCC's support of the ANC, which has a strong pro-Communist wing, would promote justice and peace in South Africa if it were to come to power.

Zimbabwe: 1979 and beyond
The WCC's commitment to the Patriotic Front in Zimbabwe was very much in evidence in 1979 when all parties to the conflict there agreed to engage in constitutional discussions at Lancaster House near London. Although the British paid the expenses of all three delegations, the WCC's Executive Committee gave the Patriotic Front delegation a special grant.

71

Its decision was based "on the fact that the gift symbolizes the WCC's longstanding commitment to seeking a negotiated and peaceful settlement in which all parties can fully participate."[27]

The WCC supported the Patriotic Front even when Mugabe and Nkomo both refused to agree to a cease-fire and demanded that their forces be fully integrated into any future Zimbabwean army. Their intransigence almost ended the talks. Prior to the Zimbabwean elections, a WCC team visiting Zimbabwe claimed to have observed "tremendous support" for the Patriotic Front. In fact, the WCC identified with the Patriotic Front so consistently that, when Mugabe won the election, he received a visiting WCC delegation and expressed his gratitude for the Council's "commitment to the principles for which you and we have struggled together."[28]

WCC staff members made no secret of their admiration for "Comrade Prime Minister Mugabe." As one remarked:

His speeches are filled with meaning and direction for Zimbabweans. For example, before the Independence Ceremony he vowed his government's commitment to peace and reconciliation. "Our new mind must have a new vision and our hearts a new love and a new spirit that must unite and not divide," he said.[29]

Furthermore, many within the WCC viewed Mugabe's victory as a vindication of their views. As a result, many of them seemed to conclude that they were beyond criticism on Zimbabwe. Philip Potter, for example, vowed at the 1980 Central Committee meeting:

We will therefore not be bullied by those who attack us for giving our attention to controversial political issues either because they claim that it detracts from the proclamation of the Gospel and the search for unity of the church or because they do not wish to be involved out of fear or indifference or a feeling of helplessness.[30]

The supposed vindication was short-lived. Only a few months after Mugabe was elected and the country's name was changed from Rhodesia to Zimbabwe, clashes between Nkomo and Mugabe supporters brought the initial glee to an abrupt end. By September 1980, Mugabe was voicing his preference for a one-party government.[31]

At the same time, heavy fighting between rival factions and irregular forces of the former guerrilla units in Matabeleland brought the country to the brink of a new civil war. This time, however, the rift was between former Patriotic Front allies Nkomo and Mugabe. Despite Nkomo's attempt to disassociate himself from the incidents, relations between him and Mugabe deteriorated rapidly. Nkomo was accused of conspiring against Mugabe, and in January 1982 he was dismissed as a government minister.

After a very difficult period of personal harassment, house arrest and even a brief period of self-imposed exile, events seemed to take a turn for the better in 1986 when Nkomo and Mugabe began "reunification" talks. These talks resulted in an agreement to the effect that Nkomo's ZAPU would merge with Mugabe's ZANU party and thus lay the foundation for the "one party" state so much desired by Mugabe. It is likely that the Soviets pressed Nkomo to reconciliation with his former rival, whom they increasingly sought to court. But this new trend had been preceded by massive bloodshed bringing the country to the brink of civil war.

A new reign of terror

The first reports of mass killings in Matabeleland by Mugabe's North Korean-trained "Fifth Brigade" army units reached the West in February 1983. One month later the *Sunday Times* of London devoted a full page to reporting the Matabeleland atrocities:

> What is happening in Matabeleland is the ugly face of Zimbabwe. Despite government denials, evidence of the army's brutality has been building up. There have been eyewitness reports, body counts, TV film, photographs, testimony from doctors, missionaries and diplomats. But this violence is matched by that of the guerrillas whose actions provoked it in the first place. White farmers in Matabeleland live in constant fear of attack by those "dissidents"— former members of Nkomo's ZAPU guerrillas, many of them deserters from the Zimbabwe army who roam the bush imposing a reign of terror. Local people speak of horrendous brutality—men buried alive, stoned to death or thrown into huts and burnt. Bodies have been found mutilated, often with lips cut off.[32]

The brutality in Matabeleland was accompanied by a crackdown on dissent within Zimbabwe, including new laws curbing press freedom. The same Mugabe who had once praised the churches' support for his struggle now responded to cautious criticism of his policies from church leaders with a demand that they "leave the government and policies well alone and stick strictly to worship."[33]

There was some sign of hope when Mugabe seemed compliant after Roman Catholic bishops and the Anglican bishop of Matabeleland called for investigations into the alleged atrocities. A WCC team that visited Zimbabwe "expressed confidence that the investigation would be thorough."[34] One year later, however, the Roman Catholic bishops' conference found it necessary to repeat its concern for the situation and claimed that thousands of Matabeleland tribe members had been murdered, raped or tortured by special army units.[35]

The turbulence also touched Mugabe's rivals. The former prime minister, Bishop Muzorewa, was arrested on 1 November 1983, on charges that he had established links with Israel and South Africa.[36]

To all of this, the WCC reacted slowly. The Council did not issue a public statement on behalf of Bishop Muzorewa, or any other of the political prisoners in Zimbabwe. When asked about the killings in Matabeleland, a WCC spokesman in July 1984 claimed that "the situation in Zimbabwe has been a matter of very serious concern for the WCC," yet:

Not all situations are necessarily dealt with by making public statements. We do not make an attempt to balance our public statements as such. A public statement has to be seen along a variety of actions that we initiate and this will include active collaboration with the churches, exploration of possibilities of how best to deal with situations in those particular contexts, in which those churches live.

In this instance, the WCC seemed to abandon its previous proclivity for public announcement:

...extensive consultations with the churches have taken place in the last few months. There have been several staff visits, major meetings of the WCC have been held, and the matter of the killings is of concern to the Council. We are in regular contact with the churches and the Zimbabwe Christian Council on that. There is no proposal at the moment for a statement on that.[37]

On the other hand, a document on "Recent Developments in Southern Africa" distributed by WCC staff among the Central Committee members in July 1984 provides an analysis of the situation in all the countries of the region—Zimbabwe included—that tends to lay the blame on one state only: South Africa. Similarly, the WCC's Vancouver Assembly referred to "clear evidence of attempts at destabilization in Zimbabwe" clearly intended "to perpetuate white dominance in the region."[38]

Although the WCC tends in other controversial situations to be highly critical of governments and the governments' version of events, in the Zimbabwe case, the WCC seems to have fully identified itself with the government in power. This is true despite the fact that Mugabe announced formation of a Soviet-style "Politburo" and is committed to a one-party dictatorship. The Mugabe government's official version of the bloody events in Zimbabwe is that opposition to its policies is inspired and supported by South Africa.

The WCC's identification with the Mugabe government became even clearer at the WCC-sponsored "emergency meeting" of about 100 international church leaders at Harare, Zimbabwe, in December 1985. Canaan Banana—a Methodist minister, president of Zimbabwe, and a close associate of Prime Minister Mugabe—presented his country as a model multiracial society. "Zimbabwe," he said, "shows that people of different races, color, and origins can live together as brothers."[39] No one at Harare criticized these words.

In justifying its grants to liberation movements such as the Patriotic Front, the WCC identified itself with "the cause of economic, social, and political justice which these organizations promote."[40] Those attending the Harare meeting fully supported "those in South Africa who are calling for the resignation of the government," and called "on the church inside and outside South Africa to support South African movements working for the liberation of their country."[41] The fact that some of these movements use violence even against civilians was deemed a necessary precondition of "liberation." Some church leaders concluded from the Harare meeting that churches should make special collections during church services and give the money to violent revolutionary movements.[42]

The concept of "reconciliation" is no longer attractive to many WCC leaders and staff members who openly espouse a violent overthrow of the present order in South Africa. This position appears in the "Kairos Document" of 1985. Although not an official statement of WCC views, the document indicates a strong current within the Council's highest levels of authority. The Kairos theologians regard any summons to reconciliation among the factions in South Africa as support for the "oppressor"

—that is, the country's white minority government. The Kairos theologians go so far as to state that pleas for reconciliation are a violation of Christian ethics, and therefore are sinful. Furthermore, the church, the document claims, "is not called to be a bastion of caution and moderation."[43]

The implication of the Kairos declaration is that those who seek a peaceful resolution of social and political strife in South Africa, most of it stemming from the government's policy of apartheid or racial separation, are guilty of sustaining both apartheid and racism. There is no longer any use, the document seems to insist, for dialogue, but only for polarization. The Kairos theologians failed to ask, however, whether casting out devils with the power of Beelzebub has worked for goodness and justice in other situations and countries. Yet radical groups that have gained governmental power elsewhere, often with WCC support, have usually instituted fresh forms of repression. The Kairos writers would have done well to ask if violent confrontation, and revolution, can bring a just new order to South Africa.

Apartheid and its structures will have to be abandoned, but it should be a peaceful transition toward a government in which both blacks and whites participate and which is formed after free and fair elections. Many blacks in South Africa oppose violence and disorder. If only those who resort to acts of violence prevail, it will be as bad for the cause of peace and justice in South Africa as would be the continuation of white minority rule.

At Odds
in the Middle East

The WCC, Israel and the PLO

The Sixth Assembly of the World Council of Churches held at Vancouver in August 1983 called for "the implementation of the rights of the Palestinians to self-determination, including the right of establishing a sovereign Palestinian state."[1] The Assembly recognized the Palestine Liberation Organization (PLO) as a party to the conflict with every right to be involved in "negotiations for a comprehensive settlement in the Middle East." The Assembly also asked the churches to remind Christians in the West "that their guilt over the fate of Jews in their countries may have influenced their views of the conflict in the Middle East and has often led to uncritical support of the policies of the state of Israel, thereby ignoring the plight of the Palestinian people and their rights."[2]

The political sympathies in the statement indicate the perspective toward the Middle East that has prevailed in the WCC during the past decade. The WCC's support for the PLO has not condoned violence in the region. On the contrary, the WCC's general secretary on three occasions in the early 1970s firmly and unequivocally denounced the use of terrorist tactics in the Middle East. In September 1970, WCC General Secretary Eugene Carson Blake wrote to the PLO's Central Committee and condemned the PLO's hijacking of civilian aircraft and the taking of innocent hostages. While expressing sympathy with the Palestinians' frustrations, and an understanding of their "desire to focus world attention on [their] situation," he urged the PLO to refrain from further acts which threatened innocent civilians.[3] A similar letter was sent to PLO leaders two years later in response to the PLO's brutal hijacking incident at Lydda Airport. The sharpest WCC criticism, however, came in response to the terrorist attack on the Israeli team at the 1972 Olympic Games at Munich. Writing the PLO committee once again, Blake denounced the killings as "senseless," and warned the PLO that "actions such as these do the greatest possible disservice to the cause of the Palestinians which your committee seeks to serve."[4]

In the same letter, however, Blake appears to be an advocate of PLO participation in international organizations: "We recognize that you have felt unjustly excluded from various governmental and international forums which have made decisions profoundly affecting your future."[5] While recognizing that the PLO was responsible for acts of terrorism, the general secretary of the WCC simultaneously made a plea for the participation of this very organization in the United Nations.

Subsequent WCC statements on the PLO showed a remarkable sympathy for the Palestinian cause. The Nairobi Assembly stressed, for example, that in order to achieve a peaceful settlement of the Arab-Israeli conflict "the rights of the Palestinian people to self-determination" must be implemented.[6]

The PLO in turn fully appreciated the WCC's concern for its cause. In November 1975 PLO Chairman Yasar Arafat sent a special message to the WCC's Nairobi Assembly, praising the WCC for making "real progress in disparting the darkness that enveloped suffering humanity" and offering the WCC "our hands in token of our readiness for cooperation, dialogue and common struggle."[7]

Some WCC officials were flattered by Arafat's charm offensive. Speaking in connection with the U.N. observance of an International Day of Solidarity with the Palestinian People in November 1982, CCIA Director Ninan Koshy referred to the PLO as "one of the most viable liberation movements in recent history in genuineness of motivation, grass roots appeal, organizational structure and international support and standing."[8]

In July 1984, a WCC delegation visited Yasir Arafat while he was in Geneva for talks with the United Nations general secretary. In the meeting, Arafat thanked the WCC for its support of the Palestinian people, especially during the Israeli invasion of Lebanon. The WCC delegation and the PLO leader also discussed the overall situation in the Middle East, and the WCC's humanitarian programs for assistance to Palestinian refugees.[9]

It is important to point out that the WCC's repeated commitment to what its 1980 Consultation on Racism called the Palestinians' "struggle to regain territory and...right of self-determination" did not mean in principle a denial of Israel's right to exist. For example, while Koshy defended the PLO, he called upon the Palestinian organization "to recognize Israel's right to exist as a state, in order to strengthen the present political momentum for achieving genuine peace."[10] In addition, the WCC's Vancouver Assembly recognized "the right of all states, including Israel and Arab states, to live in peace with secure and recognized boundaries."[11] Indeed, Potter spoke out firmly and fairly in response to the 1975 U.N. Resolution sponsored by Arab nations and the Soviet bloc that equated Zionism with racism. The WCC, Potter said, views with "deep concern" the United Nations' pronouncement. "Zionism has historically been a movement concerned with liberation of the Jewish people from oppression, including racial oppression," he insisted. Potter called on the U.N. General Assembly "to reconsider and rescind this Resolution."[12]

What the WCC's biases have meant, however, is a consistent pattern of issue-by-issue indifference or even hostility to Israeli interests. While the Council has treated with silence or euphemism the human rights violations committed by Arabs, it has often singled Israel out for specific criticism.

In 1975, the CCIA published a report of a team visit by Ninan Koshy and Stanley Mitton to Iraq. Although Iraq was notorious for its brutal suppression of the Kurds, the WCC team gave favorable assessment of Iraqi policies regarding the Kurds, particularly after the coming to power of the Baath party, which had been preceded by a "reactionary and dictatorial government."[13] At that time Iraq was a major Soviet client, receiving vast amounts of arms from the Soviet bloc. Israel with its pro-Western policy could do no good.

Typical is CCIA Director Ninan Koshy's blunt assessment in *Human Rights in the West Bank*: "For more than fifteen years the Israelis have been flying in the face of international law and public opinion by occupying and settling the West Bank...[they] are not interested in any peace plan."[14] Typical as well was the fact that the WCC Nairobi Assembly could not bring itself to endorse Secretary Potter's defense of Zionism, despite the efforts of delegations from the German Evangelical Church and the American United Presbyterian Church.[15] The only Jewish rabbi invited to participate as a guest at the assembly said afterwards that he felt completely alone at the worldwide ecumenical assembly.[16]

The question of Jerusalem

Churches from Arab countries have long exerted considerable pressure on the WCC to denounce the unification of East and West Jerusalem under Israeli rule. In its first major statement on Jerusalem in 1974, the Council's Central Committee implicitly condemned the annexation of (East) Jerusalem by Israel, stating "that matters related to jurisdiction over Jerusalem will only find their lasting solution within the context of the settlement of the conflict in its totality." The statement also suggested that "any solution on Jerusalem should take into account the rights and needs of the indigenous people of the Holy City."[17]

In 1980, the Central Committee adopted a much stronger statement on Jerusalem in opposing the "Israeli unilateral action of annexing East Jerusalem and uniting the City and its 'eternal capital' under its exclusive sovereignty." That statement called the decision "contrary to all pertinent U.N. Resolutions." The statement added that "just as the future status of Jerusalem has been considered part of the destiny of the Jewish people, so it cannot be considered in isolation from the destiny of the Palestinian people, and should thus be determined within the general context of the settlement of the Middle East conflict in its totality."[18] Although the Central Committee denied even consideration of many delegates' request that it address the annexation of an entire country—Afghanistan by the Soviet Union—it gave almost unanimous approval to a denunciation of the annexation of half a city by Israel.

Of course the Central Committee's pronouncement provoked strong reactions in Jewish circles. The International Jewish Committee for Interreligious Consultation described the statement as "political in character and flagrantly partisan" and asked the WCC "to reconsider this one-sided and biased declaration:"

> The Holy City of Jerusalem has evoked deep spiritual attachments and emotional ties for Jews, Christians and Muslims. For Jews only, however, has Jerusalem been the Eternal City, the Center of their spiritual world, and the focus of hope for millennia. For the past three thousand years, there has always been a living Jewish community in Jerusalem.[19]

The WCC and Camp David

One of the most stunning events of 1978 was the dramatic gesture of reconciliation extended to Israel by Egyptian President Anwar Sadat. A year later, the Camp David Accords signed by Sadat and Israeli Prime Minister Menachem Begin seemed to promise a peaceful solution to the Middle East question. Predictably, Sadat's initiative was opposed by radical Arab states and the PLO. Together, the radical Arabs and PLO announced formation of the "Steadfastness Front" committed to the destruction of Israel and the overthrow of the present Egyptian government by "nationalist and progressive forces" within Egypt itself. The WCC did not support Sadat, either. Indeed, many WCC policymakers were anything but enthusiastic about the Camp David agreement.

The WCC's Central Committee meeting in Jamaica in January of 1979 pointed to what it termed "unresolved conflicts in the Middle East posing serious threats to peace in the region and globally," and to "the lack of progress towards peace and negotiations involving all parties concerned including the Palestinians."[20] Whatever the statement's meaning, it certainly did not commend the successes of the Camp David peace process, or the rapprochement between Egypt and Israel. This was because the statement's drafting committee was sharply divided over the issue, as the committee's moderator, William P. Thompson, made quite clear.[21]

The Lebanese crisis

The WCC has consistently blamed Israel alone for the crisis in Lebanon. The Council's CCIA has been especially critical of Israel's policies toward Lebanon, and in 1981 called for:

> ...the termination of Israeli attacks and interventions against Lebanon and Palestinians in South Lebanon which Israel claims is necessary for its security and a help to Lebanon.

According to the CCIA, "...the security of both Israel and Lebanon depends upon Israeli recognition of Palestinian self-determination and the establishment of a just peace with the Palestinians and Arab countries in general.[22]

Nor did CCIA Director Ninan Koshy mince words when he condemned Israel's invasion of Lebanon in 1982:

> This was a premeditated, carefully planned, ruthlessly executed aggression. The objective was to exterminate Palestinian nationalism. The invasion was part of the Israeli attempt at solving the Palestinian problem by force both within the occupied territories and outside.[23]

The WCC Central Committee's response to the Israeli action in Lebanon was similar in substance, but somewhat less pointed than the CCIA's. At its Geneva meeting in July 1982, the Central Committee condemned the Israeli "siege on West Beirut" as "horrible and scandalous," and affirmed "its conviction that the recovery of Lebanese territorial integrity is a key to peace and justice in the region, and that, for this to be realized, all foreign forces must be withdrawn from Lebanese territory." The Central Committee called upon:

> ...the United Nations and all governments to treat with utmost urgency the resolution of the Palestinian question on the basis of the Palestinians' right to self-determination, including the right of establishing a sovereign Palestinian state.[24]

The committee appealed for support of "initiatives for a comprehensive settlement in the Middle East, by which the rights of Lebanon, Israel and other states of the region to live in peace within secure and recognized boundaries are guaranteed.[25]

The committee debated the proposed draft resolution. Archbishop Ajamian of the Armenian Apostolic church pointed out that Syria had played a dominant role in Lebanon since 1975, and that more than 20,000 Christians had been victims of the prolonged war there. He suggested that the Israeli invasion was not the cause but the consequence of the tragedy in which Lebanon was the victim. Norwegian delegate the Rt. Rev. Per Loenning opposed the committee's proposed reference to "a sovereign Palestinian state."[26] Committee members also discussed how to address the PLO's involvement in the fighting in Lebanon. The committee finally agreed to include the following phrase in its statement: "Even though the intention (of the Israeli incursion) may have been to destroy the PLO forces, the warfare has been directed especially against the refugee camps."[27]

The issue of terrorism
Although terrorism was one of the major international problems between 1975 and 1986, the WCC produced no significant statement condemning or analyzing the phenomenon. The Council's CCIA produced only a booklet in its "Background Information" series which explains the impact of Italian terrorism from the "uncertain" and "unproductive" strategy of the left, especially the Italian Communist Party (PCI), and the difficulties of labor unions.[28]

The topic of terrorism was conspicuous by its absence from deliberations of the WCC's Vancouver Assembly in 1983. How can this be explained? Certainly the World Council of Churches does not condone terrorism. Yet the Council has been relatively silent on the object since the WCC general secretary condemned Palestinian terrorism in the early 1970s. The explanation may be that the WCC in the 1970s expressed even more directly than before a sympathy with so-called "liberation movements" that sought the violent overthrow of established political orders. Many times the tactics of these liberation movements were difficult to distinguish from the tactics used by terrorists. There is, after all, no essential difference between a "liberation" bombing in South Africa and a "terrorist" bombing in Northern Ireland. Throughout the 1970s and early 1980s, the WCC tended to condemn violence committed by governments, but tended not to condemn violence committed against governments. On balance, the Council's position on terrorism was not much different from the Communists' view that "state terrorism" is an evil worse than individual acts of terrorism. Consequently, the Council more clearly condemned violent policies authorized by governments such as those of South Africa or Israel, but was less specific in commenting on violent acts by the African National Congress (ANC) or the PLO. Moreover, the WCC has only rarely focused attention on those countries that harbor terrorists. For example, in 1979 when the Iranians assaulted the U.S. embassy in Teheran and held scores of Americans hostage for over a year, WCC General Secretary Philip Potter twice appealed to the Ayatollah Khomeini of Iran for release of the captives. Both appeals, however, were deliberately phrased in extremely polite, even obsequious, language. For example: "We appeal to Your Eminence to show compassion and release the hostages," and "with our prayers for the people of Iran," etc.[29]

The WCC's Central Committee never issued a public statement condemning Iran for the terrorist act, nor for violating diplomatic law in occupying the American embassy. Similarly, the WCC has never condemned those countries, such as Syria and Libya, that harbored international terrorists. On the contrary, the Council tends to express an understanding of such countries.

For example, the WCC was silent in April 1986 when the United States claimed to have irrefutable evidence that Libya was directly involved in a series of terrorist attacks on American citizens, particularly in West Germany. Yet when the Untied States responded with military strikes against terrorist bases in Libya, the WCC immediately expressed through an official spokesman "profound sympathy for all those who have suffered as a result of the U.S. raid on Libya." The same spokesman said that the WCC "condemns this attack as immoral and as seriously violating laws and norms governing international relations. The WCC is deeply concerned about the spread of international terrorism, but is convinced that it cannot be solved by acts of war or violent retaliation."[30]

In addition, the WCC's office in New York City, together with the Riverside Church of New York, whose pastor at the time was the Rev. William Sloane Coffin, Jr., "Appealed to Reason" in a large advertisement in the *New York Times*, and called "the attack on Libya an attack on the soul of America."[31]

Once again, the WCC selectively criticized the United States to the extent of showing solidarity with a country—Libya—whose involvement in international terrorism is a matter of record. As long as the WCC does not produce a significant public statement on international terrorism and its linkages in the Arab world, WCC condemnations of governments responding to this major threat will only serve to further discredit the Council.

Nuclear Disarmament: Tilting Toward the Soviet Line

The WCC and the nuclear issue

Between 1975 and 1984, a number of groups lobbied the World Council of Churches to initiate a special "Program for Disarmament and Against Militarism and the Arms Race" (PDAM) patterned after the successful "Program to Combat Racism." Pressing for the program were churches from the Eastern bloc, especially the Hungarian Reformed Church and the Russian Orthodox church, and also the Prague-based Christian Peace Conference (CPC). The CPC had tried to set the tone for the WCC's Nairobi Assembly in 1975 with a statement that "strivings for the survival of humanity represent a practical ecumenism in which the question of unity is certainly not solved but nevertheless can be greatly promoted."[1]

One of the PDAM proposal's ardent supporters was Alexey Buevski, secretary of the Foreign Relations Department of the Moscow Patriarchate and a veteran spokesman on behalf of the Soviet Union's perspective at WCC Central Committee meetings. Buevski was present when the Central Committee meeting in Jamaica devoted some discussions to the PDAM. Dismissing objections made at previous ecumenical meetings by other churches' spokesmen, Buevski said that, "If there is a program which should have priority, it is the Program Against Militarism and for Disarmament. This program cannot be cut off."[2] Similar words of encouragement came from Imre Miklos, president of the Hungarian State Office for Church Affairs, when he visited the WCC's Geneva headquarters in 1978. "This developing program of the WCC," Miklos said, "can give a dynamic impetus to the churches all over the world, especially now, when every success in disarmament may mean the survival of humanity."[3]

Eastern bloc churches were joined in promoting anti-militarism policies for the WCC by several Third World churches that were pushing for regional nuclear disarmament in the Pacific. Individual delegates, such as Dutch economist H.M. de Lange, also contributed to the formation of the Program to Combat Militarism. Delegates to the WCC's Nairobi Assembly had urged churches to "make concrete the warnings they have already pronounced against militarism."[4] The same Assembly issued a statement that governments could guarantee their national security "without resorting to the use of weapons of mass destruction," and declared delegates' willingness "to live without the protection of armaments."[5]

The WCC's adoption of such positions was not due solely to lobbying efforts by outside organizations. Within the WCC itself, especially within the Department of Church and Society and the Commission on International Affairs, a number of anti-nuclear activists were at work. Without the influence of these individuals, many of them pacifists, the WCC would not have embraced the specific anti-militaristic policies that prevailed in the 1970s and early 1980s.

Toward anti-militarism

A WCC Consultation on Militarism held in Glion, Switzerland, in November 1977 found that "military forces today in both developed and developing societies sustain and promote unjust economic, social, and political structures." It said external factors promoting militarism included "the competition of the two superpowers to gain quantitative and technological arms superiority." The Consultation said the superpowers' development of first strike capabilities "bring us even nearer to the brink of a new world war," and it condemned "the frequently used argument of national security" as "no justification for this arms race."[6]

One of the principal factors that foster militarism in various countries around the world, according to the Consultation, is "the military-industrial complex." Because many in the WCC tend to link "militarism" and "capitalism" there is a tendency to primarily blame Western capitalistic countries for the arms race.[7] Accordingly, the Consultation said that there exists "a coalition between the military commanding the means of violence and the existing social and economic order," and "the rise of the 'military-industrial complex' in industrialized and developed countries, particularly where the profit motive is active."[8] A later resolution repudiated policies that "equate the defense of a particular economic and social system with that of Western/Christian civilization."[9]

The WCC returned for a second consultation on militarism to Glion in April 1978 to prepare for the United Nations' First Special Session on Disarmament scheduled later that year. This Consultation declared: "It is the prophetic duty of Christians to unmask and challenge idols of military doctrine and technology in the light of the Christian vision of justice and peace." What were these idols? One of the primary ones, according to the Consultation, is "the doctrine of deterrence which holds millions hostage to the threat of nuclear terror." The second session at Glion also declared that "there is a clear relationship between the armaments race and the socioeconomic order."[10]

WCC General Secretary Philip Potter reiterated these themes in his address to the United Nations' Special Session. He decried "the idol of a distorted concept of national security," and linked the crusade for disarmament to "the struggle for a just, participatory, and sustainable society," and a "New International Economic Order."[11]

WCC leaders were disappointed, however, in the U.N. meeting. A study by the Council's CCIA objected both to "the bellicose language of NATO leaders [which] led some observers to feel that they acted in open defiance both of the U.N. and of world public opinion," and to Soviet Foreign Minister Gromyko's comments which the CCIA study said were "practically devoid of any new proposal."[12] The WCC's own position on disarmament was to act by forming a "mobilization and education" campaign with churches playing a central role.[13] At the very least, the WCC wanted a change in the way the issue was addressed. "The concern for peace has to be articulated in elementary terms," suggested a CCIA study, "in basic propositions which are not only rationally clear but can evoke an emotional response from the people." Consequently, the CCIA recommended support for peace movements emerging around the world.[14]

In July of 1979, the WCC sponsored a conference at the Massachusetts Institute of Technology (MIT) in Cambridge, Massachusetts, on "Faith, Science, and the Future." Delegates adopted a "Science for Peace" resolution. In it, they acknowledged "with penitence the part played by science in the development of weapons of mass destruction and the failure of the churches to oppose it." The resolution recommended local and national programs to convert military research production facilities to nonmilitary, civilian use. It concluded with a pledge by signers "never again to allow science and technology to threaten the destruction of human life, and to accept the God-given task of using 'Science for Peace.'"[15]

Third World delegates to the meeting called for unilateral disarmament by the United States and the Soviet Union: "This is the only position in harmony with the Gospel, the only way out of the impasse in which we find ourselves."[16] Russian Orthodox Archbishop Kirill carefully skirted the issue. But in his conference address entitled "Major Emphases of Christian Responsibility in the Perspective of Nuclear Disarmament," he called for the "creation of regional systems of security, the creation of peace areas in different regions, stopping the supply of arms [and] the peaceful solution of local conflicts [which] can contribute to the creation of a favorable climate for disarmament." Kirill said that "one of the main problems of modern life is the question of nuclear disarmament as a concrete step towards complete and general disarmament."[17]

Roger Shinn of Union Theological Seminary in New York argued that he "would not today advocate unilateral disarmament for the Soviet Union or for my own country. My reason is not that the Russians are worse than we, but that we all have the same failings."[18] Anglican Bishop Hugh Montefiore suggested that "to keep the peace, we need to keep the balance of deterrence—though, please God, not at the present level. To lose this balance is, I believe, to bring nuclear war closer, rather than to take it further away." Bishop Montefiore hoped:

> To remove injustice, aggressiveness, unreasonableness on both sides of opposing nuclear blocs, on both sides to promote justice, understanding, détente and confidence...That seems to me the prime requisite, and it is nowhere mentioned in this draft resolution. This is the churches' prime task, as I see it, laid upon all: laid upon the churches of those belonging to countries of each opposing nuclear bloc; laid upon the churches of those who belong to neither, to those in a position of powerlessness.[19]

The WCC's Central Committee in August 1980 commended to its member churches the findings of the conference at MIT.

NATO's "Double Track" decision
In December 1979, NATO ministers approved the deployment in Europe of 464 Tomahawk cruise missiles and 108 Pershing II ballistic missiles. According to NATO, the action was purely defensive in nature:

> The Warsaw Pact has over the years developed a large and growing capability in nuclear systems that directly threaten Western Europe

and have a strategic significance for the Alliance in Europe. This situation has been especially aggravated over the last few years by Soviet decisions to implement programs modernizing and expanding their long-range nuclear capability substantially. In particular, they have developed the SS-20 missile, which offers significant improvements over previous systems in providing greater accuracy, more mobility, and greater range, as well as having multiple warheads, and the Backfire bomber, which has a much better performance than other Soviet aircraft deployment hitherto in a theater role. During this period, while the Soviet Union has been reinforcing its superiority in Long Range Theater Nuclear Forces both quantitatively and qualitatively, Western LRTNF capabilities have remained static. Indeed these forces are increasing in age and vulnerability and do not include land-based, long-range theater nuclear missile systems.[20]

Deployment of counterbalancing forces was not the only response from NATO. In a "double track" decision, deployment was linked to proposed negotiations for arms control with the objective of establishing "agreed limitations on U.S. and Soviet land-based long-range theater nuclear missile systems."[21]

The WCC soon responded to NATO's decision. Meeting in France in February 1980, the Council's Executive Committee expressed "serious concern" about the planned NATO deployment.[22] The same criticisms were included in a CCIA booklet in which CCIA Director Leopoldo Niilus put forth a position not much different from the Soviets':

> The already existing 7,000 medium-range rockets stationed in Europe sufficiently cover the Soviet deployed SS-20 missiles. Compared with about half that number of W.T.O. equivalents, they do not therefore represent a "counterforce capability." It is perhaps for this reason that the NATO decision included an offer to negotiate, which the USSR has so far rejected, because it finds itself at a strategic disadvantage in such negotiations. For the USA, middle range rockets are "tactical," because such weapons are incapable of reaching the territory of the USA. For the USSR, the same missiles are "strategic" because of its geographical proximity to Western Europe, where these are stationed (hence the term "Eurostrategic missiles"). Understandably, the Soviet Union is as nervous about such stationing as was the United States about the stationing of medium-range missiles in Cuba in the early 1960s.[23]

By August 1980, the WCC Central Committee was convinced that "the hands of the clock moved closer to the midnight of nuclear war." "The tension between the USA and the USSR has increased," the Committee commented, "heightened by the NATO decision to base new missiles possessing counterforce qualities and exceptional accuracy."[24] The Committee deliberately singled out the NATO decision. An earlier draft had been more evenhanded and had observed that "the United States and the Soviet Union seem to be ready to apply a nuclear warfighting strategy."[25] Pressured by Russian delegate Buevski, the committee altered the text. The result was the suggestion that the United States and NATO were actually contemplating "limited nuclear war."[26]

The pressure from Eastern bloc church representatives increased at the August 1981 Central Committee meeting in Dresden. A message from East German Communist party leader Erich Honecker was read which said, *inter alia*, "Your manifold activities have met with much sympathy among us."[27] Delegates from churches in the Soviet Union and Eastern Europe subsequently made it clear that the Program for Disarmament and Against Militarism was to be given the highest priority."[28]

The most substantial dividend of this pressure was the committee's lengthy statement on "Increased Threats to Peace and the Tasks for the Churches." It contained a sharp denunciation of "new dehumanizing weapons" such as the neutron bomb, which it termed "a tremendous threat because it makes the use of nuclear weapons more likely." The same statement called the U.S. neutron bomb "a further incentive to escalate the arms race." The committee also urged that "the manufacture of this and other weapons be stopped, those already produced be eliminated, and that no other nation decide to manufacture them." By contrast, the statement made no mention of Soviet weapons—especially the SS-20 missile—a sign of the influence of Eastern bloc delegates.

The statement also called on churches around the world to challenge "military and militaristic policies," and to counter what it called "the trend to characterize those of other nations and ideologies as 'the enemy' through the promotion of hatred and prejudice." Churches were also encouraged to "assist in demythologizing current doctrines of national security."[29]

Condemning nuclear weapons and "deterrence"

In late 1981, while mass demonstrations against the Pershing II and cruise missiles were being staged throughout Europe, the WCC held an International Hearing on Nuclear Weapons and Disarmament in Amsterdam. The hearing brought together theological, political and military leaders, as well as representatives of several peace movements. They were asked to speak before a carefully chosen "Hearing Group" which included church leaders —such as Bishop Karoly Toth of Hungary and Metropolitan Paulos Gregorios of India—with strong ties to the Soviet-controlled Christian Peace Conference (CPC).

The results were predictable. Peace groups pressed for a clear condemnation of both the doctrine of nuclear deterrence and the possession and use of nuclear weapons. The hearing adopted just such a policy:

> It would be an exaggeration to claim that the strategy of nuclear deterrence, and the weapons on which it depends, are as unmitigated an evil as an actual nuclear war would be. We believe, however, that they are evil, and that the possession of such weapons and the readiness to use them are wrong in the sight of God and should be treated as such by the churches.[30]

The hearing urged churches to declare unequivocally that "the production and deployment as well as the use of nuclear weapons are a crime against humanity and that such activity must be condemned on ethical and theological grounds."[31] The WCC later adopted these views officially as its own. Experts at the hearing who argued to the contrary obviously had little influence.

As an alternative to nuclear deterrence, which it called "a new form of idolatry," the hearing urged governments to adopt a policy that it defined as "common security." This proposal was developed by two members of the Independent Commission on Disarmament and Security Issues— German Social Democrat Egon Bahr and Georgi Arbatov, director of the Moscow-based Institute of the USA and Canada and a personal adviser to Soviet leader Leonid Brezhnev. The Swedish politician Olof Palme (at that time the Social Democratic opposition leader) presented the proposal which called for governments to establish their own national security by cooperating with their adversaries.[32]

In its deliberations, the hearing repeatedly blurred distinctions between East and West. Typical of the spirit in which the session was conducted were the words of the Rev. William Sloane Coffin, Jr., then of the Riverside Church, New York City, who opened the hearing:

> Were we truly to hear Jesus' words, Soviet missiles would remind us of nothing so much as our own; Soviet threats to rebellious Poles

would call to mind American threats to rebels in El Salvador; and Afghanistan would prompt us to remember Vietnam.[33]

The WCC Central Committee supported the Amsterdam hearing's findings when it met at Geneva in 1982, and underscored the hearing's conclusion that "the production and deployment, as well as the use, of nuclear weapons are a crime against humanity." Such a view, the committee stated, "should become an official position for churches and Christians."[34]

The Central Committee also "received with appreciation" a report on PDAM that recommended that disarmament be addressed from a perspective broader than the East-West confrontation: "Not only militarism and the arms race, but also social injustice, economic deprivation, political repression, and environmental devastation have to be exposed as factors undergirding the present peaceless global system."[35] CPC President Karoly Toth was among those who stressed the importance of PDAM: "Work on the issue of militarism was extremely important."[36]

The committee's final action at Geneva in 1982 was to reiterate its support for "the growing number of peace and disarmament movements in different parts of the world." In addition, the panel called on churches "to intensify their efforts...to mobilize a forceful world public opinion by deepening their analysis of the issues and understanding of the political struggle, and by promoting unity among groups with different viewpoints who share a common desire for peace and disarmament."[37]

Peace and security issues at Vancouver

The theme of the WCC's 1983 Vancouver Assembly—"Jesus Christ: The Life of the World"—gave delegates ample opportunity to raise issues of peace and national security. To insure that direct discussions of these issues took place, WCC staff members invited the highly controversial theologian Dorothee Soelle to address the Assembly. Her speech, entitled "Life in Its Fullness," charged that the West is "under the domination of NATO." She denounced militarism as "humanity's supreme effort to get rid of God once and for all."[38] In a subsequent press conference, Soelle praised Karl Marx and predicted violent clashes in West Germany if the West German government permitted deployment of new NATO missiles.

These same themes were echoed by one of the Assembly's most prominent issue groups, called "Confronting Threats to Peace and Survival." Chaired by Paulos Mar Gregorios of India, a longtime Christian Peace Conference

(CPC) associate, the group urged that the West's nuclear deterrence doctrine be "categorically rejected as contrary to our faith in Jesus Christ." The group labelled deterrence "morally unacceptable because it relies on the credibility of the intention to use nuclear weapons: we believe that any intention to use weapons of mass destruction is an utterly inhuman violation of the mind and spirit of Christ which should be in us."[39] The group reached the same conclusions as the Amsterdam Hearing:

> Only a common enterprise undertaken by all the nations of the world together can ensure dependable international security. No nation can achieve security at the expense of others, through seeking military superiority or interfering in the life of other nations. Deterrence or peace by terror should give place to the concept of common security for all, which includes people's security in each nation.[40]

The only moderate words in the report were included at the insistence of delegates who argued that a complete denunciation of deterrence doctrine would alienate many Christians and churches. After all, these delegates pointed out, Pope John Paul II had previously declared that nuclear deterrence based on balance as a step on the way to progressive disarmament could be viewed as morally acceptable. Consequently, the Assembly acknowledged that "many Christians and others sincerely believe that deterrence provides an interim assurance of peace and stability on the way to disarmament." The Assembly further stated that "we must work together with those advocates of interim deterrence who are earnestly committed to arms reduction." Nevertheless, "the cruel illusions of such faith in deterrence" have been exposed.[41]

The Vancouver Assembly produced its own "Statement on Peace and Justice," based largely on findings of previous WCC meetings and the report of the "Confronting Threats to Peace and Survival" issues group. The Assembly statement reiterated themes of previous WCC meetings, and emphasized the relationship to justice of national concerns for peace and security:

> No nation can pretend to be secure so long as others' legitimate rights to sovereignty and security are neglected and denied. Security can be achieved only as a common enterprise of nations, but security is also inseparable from justice. A concept of "common security" of nations must be reinforced by a concept of "people's security." True security for the people demands respect for human rights, includ-

ing the right to self-determination, as well as social and economic justice for all within every nation, and a political framework that would ensure it.[42]

The Assembly's final statement also called on churches in Europe—both East and West—and in North America "to redouble their efforts to convince their governments to reach a negotiated settlement to turn away now, before it is too late, from plans to deploy additional or new nuclear weapons in Europe, and to begin immediately to reduce and then eliminate altogether present nuclear forces."[43]

One of the most outspoken critics of the WCC's condemnation of nuclear deterrence was the archbishop of York, Dr. John Hab good. Habgood had presided over the Amsterdam Hearing in 1981. He felt that it would not be right for Christians to think that there were quick and easy answers to complex issues like the nuclear balance.

The purpose of deterrence is to have weapons in order to prevent war. The intention of deterrence is good. The possession of nuclear weapons, although undesirable, is not as evil as their actual use will be.[44]

After Vancouver the theme "Justice, Peace and the Integrity of Creation" became dominant in ecumenical discussions. A major world conference on this theme is planned for 1990. But so far, preparations for this event have been rather poor.

The 1987 Treaty on the Elimination of Intermediate Range and Shorter Range Missiles (INF) between the United States and the Soviet Union, was much welcomed in WCC circles. Many in the WCC felt vindicated in their views on nuclear disarmament. They failed to recognize however, that the foundations for the INF Treaty had not been laid by nuclear pacificism or unilateral steps by the West. Rather, it was Western insistence that peace in Europe can best be maintained when there is nuclear stability, that is, when existing nuclear imbalances are reduced.

New Directions
for the WCC

The political transformation of theology

It is well known that totalitarian regimes manipulate the United Nations for propaganda purposes. In a truly representative international body, this is probably inevitable. As has been pointed out by Daniel Patrick Moynihan, Democratic U.S. senator from New York and former U.S. ambassador to the United Nations: "In the United Nations, there are in the range of two dozen democracies; totalitarian Communist regimes and assorted ancient and modern despotisms make up all the rest."[1]

But while governments can be expected to manipulate a political organization, churches should be expected to operate differently within an international body ostensibly intended to further the Gospel of Jesus Christ, and to foster church unity worldwide. Unfortunately, too many member churches are not beyond attempting to manipulate the World Council of Churches to their own purposes. In too many instances, WCC member churches, willingly or unwillingly, parrot within the WCC the political perspectives of their governments. In addition, WCC staff members often take one-sided political positions and have shown to be susceptible to propaganda efforts on the part of left-wing totalitarian governments. For this reason, the WCC has often more resembled a political organization than a religious body.

The WCC finds it hard to acknowledge that a number of its member churches are merely mouthpieces for governments and their political ideologies. The operating assumption of the organization is that each church speaks with its own authority. Indeed, the worldwide ecumenical movement could otherwise not hope to survive. In assuming that each member church shares equal validity, the WCC ascribes to each church's policies an equal weight.

This fiction of independence has an even worse effect to the extent that it is partially true. That is, it is true that many WCC member churches, especially those from the West, speak for themselves, and are free of governmental allegiances or interference. But this very fact only complicates the evaluation of World Council affairs and policies. For, while the Western churches are free to oppose their own secular governments, most churches from other parts of the world, especially from the Eastern bloc, are not.

For example, when the North Atlantic Treaty Organization (NATO) decided a few years ago to improve its missile defense system in Western Europe—in direct response to an increased Soviet threat—many churches in the West protested. By contrast, most Eastern bloc churches, and especially the Russian Orthodox church, had hailed as "peace policy" the Soviet military buildup that prompted the NATO response. Similarly, many American and Western European churches were vocal critics of the U.S. involvement in the Vietnam War during the 1960s and 1970s. By contrast again, Eastern bloc churches not only were not free to criticize the Soviet Union's 1979 invasion of Afghanistan, but many of them even commended both the invasion and the continued occupation.

The simple fact is that Eastern bloc churches within the WCC provide services for their governments that would be inconceivable for churches in the West. The Russian Orthodox church has sponsored—to take only one example—a number of major conferences for religious leaders "to save mankind from nuclear catastrophe." The Soviet Communist Party and state had a deep interest in these meetings. Being highly supportive of official "peace policy" their propagandistic value was enormous.

Most Eastern churches' subservience to their governments accounts to some degree for the consistently pro-Soviet bias within the World Council of Churches. The organizations' ranks include a permanently and implacably anti-Western contingent. In addition, for whatever reasons, many Western churches are either sympathetic with, or acquiesce to, the Eastern churches' relentless criticism of Western governments—especially the United States. Many key WCC staff members are sympathetic with revolutionary political ideologies. These staff members place their commitment to ideology above their fidelity to ecumenical unity, working and compromising with groups and churches controlled by the Soviet Union's propaganda apparatus. The Christian Peace Conference (CPC) headquartered in Prague is a prime example of such a group.

Since 1961 when the powerful Russian Orthodox church joined the WCC, churches or church groups from the Eastern bloc have exerted a de facto veto power when complaints arise within the WCC about policies of Eastern bloc governments. In the ensuing quarter-century, the WCC has been unable to issue effective statements about alleged human rights violations, or religious repression, in Eastern bloc states, or about Communist ideology in general.

In addition, some Third World churches, or rather radicalized elites within those churches, exerted a disproportionate influence on the policy and direction of the WCC. Liberation theology, with its positive assessment of Marxist ideology, became the dominant trend. Consequently, the WCC has failed to distance itself clearly from Marxist inspired Third World revolutionary movements. This explains why the question of totalitarianism is treated in a rather one-sided way. Since the mid-1960s the question of the totalitarian nature of Marxism has not been the subject of serious reflection within the WCC.

The human rights debate

Between 1975 and 1986 the WCC preferred to keep its friendly channels to the state-supported Russian Orthodox hierarchy open, rather than to publicize the often tragic fate of the hierarchy's critics. The voice of independent-minded Christians in the Soviet Union was suppressed at major ecumenical meetings like the Vancouver Assembly. Russian or Eastern bloc churches thwarted most attempts to adopt resolutions or issue statements about the fate of independent Christians in the Soviet Union. The few WCC pronouncements that were approved speak only of a vague "concern" about "situations." As one of the independent Russian Christians, Deacon Vladimir Rusak, wrote in a public letter to the WCC's 1983 Vancouver Assembly: "It is very difficult to reach you—much, much more difficult than to reach God."[2]

Even when reached by independent voices from the Soviet Union, WCC leaders indulge in procedural diversions and respond weakly and only after key churches exert tremendous pressure within Council deliberations. By contrast, the WCC is quick to condemn human rights abuses in countries governed by right-wing regimes.

According to Erich Weingartner, executive director of the WCC's Commission of the Churches on International Affairs (CCIA), most criticism about human rights conditions in the Soviet Union arises from Western churches in the grip of a "Cold War mentality."[3] No corresponding explanation is offered by the WCC of Eastern bloc or Third World churches' criticism of human rights conditions in, say, South Africa or Central America.

Amazingly, some WCC leaders have said they doubt the validity of complaints about religious repression or human rights violations in the Soviet Union, even those from independent Russian Christians or churches. WCC General Secretary Philip Potter said that, "It is difficult to verify whether those letters are real or whether they are part of propaganda warfare." Potter's reference is to letters protesting Soviet policy, and appealing for WCC intervention, from independent Christians within the Soviet Union.[4] Other WCC officials have said that churches from the Third World have complained about what they term "disproportionate attention" given by the Council to conditions in Eastern Europe.[5] It is not unfair to ask in reply whether WCC attention to conditions in South Africa—albeit a legitimate and understandable concern for the Council—has not by the same standards been even more "disproportionate."

WCC leaders often defend their silence about alleged problems in Eastern bloc or Third World countries with left-wing regimes and their constant criticism of Western and especially U.S. actions by claiming that the WCC can act or make pronouncements only with the permission of member churches from the country under review. For example, the WCC did not initially protest atrocities of the Idi Amin regime in Uganda during the 1970s because churches in Uganda reportedly preferred that the Council not address the issue. The WCC finally spoke openly after the murder of the Ugandan churches' leader, Archbishop Luwuum. While the WCC's policy of selective protest may have a certain utility, there is no validity to the suggestion expressed by Potter, that churches ought to have "some understanding for this brutal conduct (by Idi Amin) on the part of a nation which has only just gained independence."[6] Moreover, the WCC does not always respect the wishes of local ecumenical bodies or churches concerning Council pronouncements about international issues. A prime example of this dichotomy between expressed policy and actual practice was the WCC denunciation of the U.S. military action in Grenada in 1983. The United States claimed that it acted at the request of several other Caribbean governments and the governor-general of Grenada, Sir Paul Scoon. Its action was hailed by the Grenadian Council of Churches. Nonetheless, the WCC condemned the action.[7]

The WCC defends its so-called "silent diplomacy" toward Eastern bloc and many Third World countries by suggesting that public pronouncements would jeopardize both the Council's effectiveness and member churches in the countries involved. Weingartner even remarked that, "It will never be known to what extent the human rights debate between East and West (at the 1975 Nairobi Assembly, prompted by the Yakunin-Regelson letter from the Soviet Union) threatened substantially the WCC's human rights endeavors."[8] But the WCC does not practice silent diplomacy toward Western governments, nor does it acknowledge the propriety of silent diplomacy when practiced by Western governments. For example, the WCC has constantly criticized the United States for its "silent diplomacy" toward reforms in South Africa, especially toward elimination of the system of apartheid. It has also criticized U.S. attempts and pressure to achieve democracy in El Salvador and other Central American countries.

The bitter irony of the WCC's human rights policy is that it tended to fall silent at precisely those times when those complaining about alleged persecution—Russian dissidents or peaceful opposition groups inside Nicaragua, for example—preferred that the WCC were outspoken.

The impact of liberation theology

It is no exaggeration to say that "liberation theology" is now dominant within the World Council of Churches. It has even superseded the WCC's original emphasis on doctrine and ecclesiastical unity which is inherent to the "Faith and Order" program. Indeed, liberation theology is a manifestation of the transformation of the WCC from an ecclesiastical to a political organization.

Liberation theology, which arose within Third World circles during the late 1960s and blossomed during the 1970s, espouses political, social or economic "liberation" at all costs—including the cost of violent revolution. This theology of liberation is profoundly similar in its ideological aims and methods to Marxism; both blame social and political problems of today on the industrialized, capitalistic systems of the West. The West is held the source of militarism, racism and the political, social or economic problems in the East and the Third World. The *World Marxist Review*, a major outlet of the Soviet Communist party's International Department, nowadays champions liberation theology. It carried an appraisal of liberation theology claiming that atheists, Marxists and religious people of all kinds can, and must, form a united front against imperialism.[9]

As a theology of the political Left (revolution) but not the political Right (traditionalism), liberation theology cannot sympathize with resistance to totalitarian Communist regimes, or Communist aggression. Thus, the WCC's 1983 Vancouver Assembly proposed that outside governments —implying especially the United States—stop supplying arms to the Afghans fighting Soviet troops who invaded their country in 1979. No similar proposals were heard during the Vietnam War, when the North Vietnamese trained and armed the Communist Vietcong guerrillas in south South Vietnam. Indeed, because the WCC now deemed left-wing movements just, it has given them vast ecumenical support, both politically and financially.

A conspicuous example of the WCC's sympathy with so-called liberation movements was the WCC-sponsored "emergency meeting" on South Africa held in Harare, Zimbabwe, in December 1985. At the meeting, WCC leaders again expressed full support for liberation movements in Africa and around the world—even if those movements were to use violence. Voicing the opinion of many at Harare, South African Desmond Tutu reportedly said that the use of force to overthrow the present South African order was "justifiable."[10] The WCC believes left wing liberation movements should be given as much support as possible. Of course, the WCC, claiming its aid is purely humanitarian, declines to be officially involved in any transfer of arms. But when it comes to Afghanistan, the same WCC calls for a stop to the flow of arms to those who resist illegal occupation by a foreign invader.

WCC General Secretary Philip Potter has attempted to justify the WCC's contradictory policy by calling Afghanistan a "pagan country" beyond the Council's purview.[11] Yet no WCC general secretary has ever called the Palestinians "pagan" and dismissed their cause as a result. The Vancouver Assembly even called for the creation of a "sovereign Palestinian state." The same assembly declared that the Palestine Liberation Organization (PLO), which is condemned as a terrorist organization by a number of Western governments, should be involved in "negotiations for a comprehensive settlement in the Middle East."[12] On the other hand, the Afghanistan issue is put in quite a different perspective. The Afghan resistance is not invited to participate in "an overall political settlement" which the Vancouver Assembly recommended in the case of Afghanistan.[13]

There is good reason to question whether the WCC is serious about combatting the evils of racism and injustice. While the Council applies "just war" criteria to leftist insurgents, it denies a similar justification to movements resisting Communist aggression. In Vietnam and Nicaragua, for example, the WCC immediately fell silent about social and political conditions as soon as revolutionary regimes assumed power. By contrast, the WCC has never produced a full, public statement on human rights in Afghanistan—a country ravaged by over 100,000 troops.

WCC statements on Central America have criticized only American policy in the region. Indeed, the WCC tends to disregard and even condemn the United States' diplomatic efforts to foster democratic order in Central American countries. Reserving for itself the propriety of using "silent diplomacy," the WCC has never publicly acknowledged the constructive achievements of U.S. policy throughout the region. Instead, the Council tends to highlight U.S. policy mistakes in Central America, and therefore leaves the impression of a bias against the United States.

Suggestions for improvement
From the perspective of the present study, there are several changes in policy and practice that would enable the World Council and its member churches to make a more responsible contribution to international affairs.

First, the WCC should be more balanced in selecting individuals for key staff positions. Because the staff at WCC headquarters in Geneva, Switzerland, enjoy sweeping institutional powers, these employees must be seen as diverse, in theological and political perspectives, as the member churches' constituencies that they serve.

Second, the WCC should distance itself from known front organizations of the Soviet Communist party. Although WCC officials deny it, Soviet fronts have played a role in influencing WCC positions. Council staff members have shown a clear sympathy for one or even more of these fronts; to be both balanced and credible, the Council should break these affiliations.

Third, the WCC should be more objective in appraising the policies of Western democracies, and less uncritical of left wing revolutionary movements and totalitarian regimes. This is not to suggest that the WCC merely shift its bias from left to right; rather, it is to recommend that the WCC affirm the superiority of freedom to totalitarianism, and recognize the achievements of the world's parliamentary democracies.

Fourth, the WCC should be more modest in making pronouncements about complex international issues. By being too sweeping in its statements, the Council has contributed to the politicization of theology and to polarization of its member churches. As one of Germany's best theologians, Helmut Thielicke, once said, "While the goal of preaching can never be too high, since it is the eschatological Kingdom of God, the goal of counsel can never be too modest."[14]

Fifth, the WCC should pay stricter attention to the theological and spiritual dimensions of international affairs, and base its contribution to the international community squarely upon the unique virtues of the Judeo-Christian moral tradition. After all, as an organization of Christian churches, the WCC ought to be especially equipped to emphasize the biblical wisdom that could make such an important difference in many conflicts around the world. Moreover, fidelity to the biblical tradition would remind the WCC, and through its efforts the world at large, that no society can be effectively changed, and no just order established, unless human nature itself is regenerated in spirit. In other words, it is the biblical view that social and political conditions can be changed only when the people involved in them are changed first; the opposite view is espoused primarily by Marxist ideology, which holds that social and political problems derive not from human nature, but from social and political situations.

Too many WCC pronouncements also ignore the biblical emphasis on genuine reconciliation and forgiveness. Instead, by identifying too closely with revolutionary violence and Marxist causes, the WCC often embraces action in direct opposition to the biblical tradition.

Sixth, the WCC should renounce its support of so-called liberation movements that result in new forms of oppression rather than democratic systems and societies. According to the Judeo-Christian moral tradition, a people may justly resort to violence only in self-defense. This is precisely the situation in Afghanistan today, yet the WCC failed to recognize the just cause of the Afghan resistance fighters. But other liberation movements, many of them Marxist-inspired, received full ecumenical backing.

Seventh, and finally, the World Council of Churches should restore ideological balance to its many legitimate and commendable concerns. The Council's concern for Third World poverty, economic debt, hunger and racism, for example, is a valuable addition to the international attempts to aid millions of people. But to blame reflexively the West in general, and democratic capitalism in particular, for problems in the Third World is both unworthy of a worldwide church organization and unproductive toward resolving Third World ills.

At present, the World Council of Churches does not have such a balanced, biblical approach to international issues. Whether the WCC can return to its foundations, and restore objectivity and integrity to its analysis of political and social issues, is a question which awaits the answer only Council leaders can give.

Notes

Introduction: pp. 1-7

1. Philip Potter, *What in the World Is the World Council of Churches?* (Geneva: World Council of Churches, 1978), p. 8.

2. More background on the IMC, which was the first major international ecumenical organization of the twentieth century, can be found in: William Richey Hogg, *Ecumenical Foundations: A History of the International Missionary Council and Its Nineteenth-Century Background* (New York: Harper and Brothers Publishers, 1952).

3. Leonard Hodgson, ed., *The Second World Conference on Faith and Order, Edinburgh, 1937* (London: SCP Press, 1938), p. 151.

4. *The WCC*, information leaflet (Geneva: World Council of Churches, undated), p. 10.

5. See O. Frederick Nolde, *Freedom's Charter: The Universal Declaration of Human Rights* (New York: Foreign Policy Association, 1949), p. 5; and O. Frederick Nolde, *Human Rights and the UN: Appraisal and Next Steps* (New York: The Academy of Political Science, Columbia University, 1953), p. 39; and Harold E. Fey, ed., *The Ecumenical Advance: A History of the Ecumenical Movement*, vol. 2, 1948-1968 (London: SPCK, 1970), pp. 265, 270.

6. Eugene Carson Blake, "The World Council of Churches: East-West Church Relations 1966-1972," in *Voices of Unity*, ed. Ans J. van der Bent (Geneva: World Council of Churches, 1981), pp. 8, 9.

7. See *Soviet International Fronts*, Department of State Publication 9360 (Washington D.C., August 1983).

8. *Nuevo El Plata*, Montevideo newspaper, 4 February 1970, p. 4.

9. *World Public Opinion and the Second Special Session of the United Nations General Assembly Devoted to Disarmament. Final Report of the Conference Convened by the Special NGO Committee on Disarmament* (Geneva, 31 March-2 April 1982), p. 4.

10. Cf. *de Volkskrant*, Amsterdam daily newspaper, 19 May 1984, p. 19.

The Soviet Bloc: A "Selective Silence": pp. 9-25

1. *Target*, 25 November 1975, p. 4.

2. Ibid.

3. *Ecumenical Press Service*, 18 May 1972.

4. Ibid.

5. *One World* (July 1981), p. 19.

6. John Bluck, World Council of Churches director of communications, in *Ecumenical Press Service*, 6-10 June 1983.

7. World Council of Churches Nairobi Assembly, 1975, author's observations and notes.

8. David M. Paton., ed., *Breaking Barriers: Nairobi 1975* (London: SPCK and Geneva: World Council of Churches, 1976), p. 169.

9. Ibid.

10. Ibid., p. 174.

11. World Council of Churches Nairobi Assembly plenary debate, 9 December 1975, author's records.

12. U.S. Congress, House Select Committee on Intelligence, *Soviet Covert Action— The Forgery Offensive: Hearings Before the Subcommittee on Oversight of the Permanent Select Committee on Intelligence*, 96th Cong., 2nd sess., 1980, p. 79. Also U.S. Congress, House Select Committee on Intelligence, *The CIA and the Media: Hearings Before the Subcommittee on Oversight of the Permanent Select Committee on Intelligence*, 95th Cong., 1st and 2nd sess., p. 606.

13. Helene Posdeeff, "Die Rolle des Moskauer Patriarchats in Nairobi" in Ulrich Betz and Peter Beyerhaus, *Oekumene im Spiegel von Nairobi 1975* (Bad Liebenzell: Verlag der Liebenzeller Mission, 1976), p. 247. Also information provided to author by Professor Helene Posdeeff, a Russian Orthodox Sovietologist who attended the Nairobi Assembly.

14. Nairobi Assembly plenary debate, 9 December 1975, author's records. Also text of statement submitted to the Assembly by the Russian Orthodox Church in: Paton, *Breaking Barriers*, p. 172.

15. *The Journal of the Moscow Patriarchate* no. 4 (1976): p. 16.

16. Helene Posdeeff, "Geneva: The Defense of Believers' Rights" in *Religion in Communist Lands* No. 4 (1976): p. 5; Michael Bourdeaux, Hans Hebly, and Eugen Voss, *Religious Liberty in the Soviet Union* (Keston/Kent: Keston College, 1976), p. 52.

17. Montreux Memorandum in "The Churches and Religious Liberty in the Helsinki Signatory States," *CCIA Newsletter* no. 4 (1976): p. 17.

18. Ibid., p. 20.

19. Ibid.

20. Document no. 6, World Council of Churches Central Committee, Geneva, August 1976, p. 6.

21. Ibid., p. 5.

22. World Council of Churches Central Committee plenary sessions, Geneva, 11 August 1976, author's records.

23. Document no. 40, World Council of Churches Central Committee, Jamaica, January 1979, p. 11.

24. Imre Miklos, "Some Experience of the Policy Regarding Churches in the Hungarian People's Republic." Paper presented at the Ecumenical Center, Geneva, 27 October 1978, p. 10. Mimeo.

25. *Ecumenical Press Service*, 7 February 1980.

26. Ibid., 16 June 1977.

27. *The Journal of the Moscow Patriarchate* no. 8 (1976): p. 51.

28. *News From the USSR*, 30 May 1983, (Embassy USSR, The Hague).

29. *The Journal of the Moscow Patriarchate* no. 7 (1982): p. 63.

30. J.A. Hebly, "The Captive Churches and the Ecumenical Movement," in *Briefing Paper of the Institute on Religion and Democracy* (January 1984).

31. Ibid., p. 7.

32. *One World* (July-August 1983): p. 9.

33. Jane Ellis, "The Christian Committee for the Defense of Believers' Rights in the USSR," in *Religion in Communist Lands* vol. 8, no. 4 (1980): p. 280.

34. "Study Paper on Religious Liberty," in *CCIA Background Information* no. 4 (1980): p. 63; Minutes of the World Council of Churches Central Committee Meeting, Geneva, 1980, p. 63.

35. Michael Bourdeaux, interview with author, Keston College, Kent, England, 24 November 1980. Also J.A. Hebly, "World Council Put Under Pressure to Write Letter About Dissidents," in *Trouw*, 21 November 1980. Also *Church Times*, 29 August 1980, 5 September 1980, and 12 September 1980.

36. Full text in *Ecumenical Press Service,* 30 October 1980, pp. 3, 4. Also, Ibid., 2 October, 1980. p. 2.

37. Full text in *Ecumenical Press Service,* 13 November 1980, pp. 8, 9.

38. *The Journal of the Moscow Patriarchate,* no. 7 (1983): p. 37; and no. 8 (1983): p. 66.

39. *The Economist's Foreign Report,* 28 June 1984.

40. Translated from the Russian by Keston College, Kent, England, 2 August 1983. The German text is in *Glaube in der Zweiten Welt* no. 11 (1983): pp. 19, 20.

41. Ibid.

42. Vancouver Assembly, press conference, 8 August 1983, author's records.

43. World Council of Churches, *Reports of the Churches in International Affairs, 1979-1982* (Geneva: World Council of Churches, 1983), p. 107.

44. David Gill, ed., *Gathered for Life: Official Report of the Sixth Assembly of the World Council of Churches, Vancouver, 1983* (Grand Rapids: William B. Eerdmans, 1983), p. 142.

45. Ibid., p. 139.

46. Ibid., p. 140.

Monitoring Human Rights in Asia: pp. 27-37

1. World Council of Churches, *Reports of the Churches in International Affairs, 1970-1973* (Geneva: World Council of Churches, 1974), p. 175.

2. Ibid., p. 179.

3. World Council of Churches, *Reports of the Churches in International Affairs, 1974-1978* (Geneva: World Council of Churches, 1979), p. 152.

4. Ibid.

5. *Europa van Morgen,* 2 March 1983, p. 151.

6. *Neue Zuercher Zeitung,* 23 April 1982; U.S. Department of State, "Forced Labor in the USSR: Report to the Congress" (Washington D.C.: Department of State), 9 February 1983. Mimeo.

7. *Der Spiegel,* 4 December 1978; *U.S. News and World Report,* 27 November 1978; *Newsweek,* 18 June and 2 July 1979; *Time,* 11 December 1979.

8. David B. Barratt, ed., *World Christian Encyclopedia* (Oxford and New York, 1982), p. 746; *Herder Korrespondenz* (August 1982): p. 393, and (April 1981): p. 203; *Religion in Communist Lands* no. 1 (1982): p. 54, and numerous newspaper reports.

9. Paton, *Breaking Barriers*, p. 106.

10. *NRC Handelsbad*, 22 September 1976; *Nederlands Dagblad*, 23 September 1976.

11. *Ecumenical Press Service*, 9 June 1977.

12. Paton, *Breaking Barriers*, p. 98.

13. Ibid., pp. 100, 117.

14. World Council of Churches, *Minutes and Report of the 1973 Bangkok Assembly of the Commission on World Mission and Evangelism* (Geneva: World Council of Churches, 1973), p. 90; *International Review of Missions* vol. 62: no. 246 (1973): p. 181.

15. Philip Potter, World Council of Churches general secretary at press conference, Geneva, 9 August 1976, author's records.

16. Erich Weingartner, "Human Rights on the Ecumenical Agenda," in *CCIA Background Information* no. 3 (1983): pp. 31, 40.

17. The presentation was called "Massacre of the Innocents." Also *One World* (July/August 1983): p. 7.

18. Minutes of the World Council of Churches Central Committee Meeting, Jamaica, 1979, p. 72. Also *The Ecumenical Review* Vol. 31: no. 2 (1979): p. 195.

19. Victor Hsu, "The Indochina Conflicts: Basic Elements" in *CCIA Background Information* no. 3 (1980): p. 5.

20. Ibid., p. 28.

21. World Council of Churches, *Reports of the Churches in International Affairs, 1979-1982* (Geneva: World Council of Churches, 1983), p. 100.

22. *Report of an Ecumenical Consultation on Reconstruction and Reconciliation in Indochina* (Bangkok: The Fund for Reconstruction and Reconciliation in Indochina, 1975), pp. 50, 75.

23. *Ecumenical Press Service*, 21 June 1979.

24. Document No. 2.3, World Council of Churches Central Committee, Dresden, August 1981, p. 1.

25. Draft text of Document no. 2.3 (Doc. no. 2.2.1), World Council of Churches Central Committee, Dresden, 1981, p. 2. Also *Ecumenical Review* vol. 33: no. 4 (1981): p. 388.

26. World Council of Churches Central Committee plenary debate, Dresden, 33: no. 4 (1981): 25 August 1981, author's records.

27. *Ecumenical Press Service*, 8 May 1980.

28. World Council of Churches, *Minutes and Report of the 1973 Bangkok Assembly*, p. 32.

29. Werner Schilling, "Das Raetsel der Oekumenischen Mao-Begeisterung," in *Reich Gottes oder Weltgemeinschaft?*, ed. P. Beyerhaus and W. Kuenneth (Bad Liebenzell: Verlag de Liebenzeller Mission, 1975), pp. 155, 156.

30. Dirk Bergvelt and Charlotte van Rappart, eds., *De Papieren Lente: Documenten van de Chinese Democratische Beweging 1978-1980* (Utrecht and Antwerp: Het Spectrum, 1982), pp. 81, 134.

31. World Council of Churches, *Reports of the Churches in International Affairs, 1979-1982*, p. 107.

32. Ibid., p. 108; *Ecumenical Press Service*, 29 May 1980; *One World* (July 1980): p. 14.

33. Leopoldo Niilus, introduction to "Human Rights in the Republic of Korea" in *CCIA Background Information* no. 1 (1979): p. 2.

34. *Ecumenical Press Service*, 22 September 1977.

35. World Council of Churches, *Reports of the Churches in International Affairs, 1979-1982*, p. 106.

36. Leopoldo Niilus, introduction to "Iron Hand, Velvet Glove," in *CCIA Background Information* no. 2 (1980): p. 2.

37. Gill, *Gathered for Life*, p. 166.

38. *Washington Post*, 25 February 1986.

"Threats to Peace": Conflict and Compromise: pp. 39-50

1. *Ecumenical Press Service*, 21 February 1980.

2. Minutes of the World Council of Churches Central Committee Meeting, Toronto, 1950, p. 91.

3. William C. Fletcher, *Religion and Soviet Foreign Policy 1945-1970*, (London: Oxford University Press, 1973), p. 117.

4. *Ecumenical Press Service*, 29 August 1968.

5. *Journal of the Moscow Patriarchate* no. 5 (1980): p. 5.

6. For background information on the World Council of Churches and liberation theology see: Ernest W. Lefever, *Amsterdam to Nairobi: The World Council of Churches and the Third World* (Washington: Ethics and Public Policy Center, 1979), p. 30; Beyerhaus and Kuenneth, *Reich Gottes oder Weltgemeinschaft?*, pp. 88, 130.

7. World Council of Churches, *Your Kingdom Come: Report on the World Conference on Mission and Evangelism, Melbourne, May 1980* (Geneva: World Council of Churches, 1980), p. 242.

8. World Council of Churches' World Conference on Mission and Evangelism, Melbourne, May 1980, author's record, including information provided by delegates.

9. Author's record of information provided by Professor Helene Posdeeff of the Russian Orthodox Church. Also Posdeeff, "Die Rolle des Moskauer Patriarchats," p. 247.

10. Melbourne Conference plenary debate, 23 May 1980, author's record.

11. Ibid., 24 May 1980.

12. World Council of Churches, *Your Kingdom Come*, p. 247.

13. World Council of Churches Central Committee plenary debate, Geneva, 21 August 1980, author's record.

14. Ibid.

15. Philip Potter, interview with author, Geneva, 22 August 1980. The text of the interview was later screened by the World Council of Churches and published in *Reformatorisch Dagblad*, a Christian daily newspaper in Apeldoorn, The Netherlands, 3 September 1980.

16. Author's record of World Council of Churches Central Committee plenary debate, Geneva, 15 August 1980.

17. Text is in World Council of Churches, *Reports of the Churches in International Affairs, 1979-1982*, p. 45; and Minutes of the World Council of Churches Central Committee Meeting, Geneva, 1980, p. 64.

18. Philip Potter, interview with author, Geneva, 22 August 1980.

19. U.S. Congress, House Subcommittee on Oversight of the Permanent Select Committee on Intelligence, *Hearings on Soviet Covert Action*, 96th Cong., 2nd sess., 6 and 19 February 1980, pp. 59, 79.

20. *Ecumenical Press Service,* 4 September 1980.

21. Ibid.

22. Gill, *Gathered For Life,* p. 161.

23. Document no. 2-11, World Council of Churches' Sixth Assembly, Vancouver, 1983, p. 10.

24. Vancouver Assembly plenary debate, 9 August 1983, author's record.

25. *Canvas,* daily newspaper of the World Council of Churches' Sixth Assembly, Vancouver, 1983, 9 August 1983, p. 2. Also Vancouver Assembly plenary debate, 9 August 1983, author's record.

26. Translated from the Russian in author's record of Vancouver Assembly plenary debate, 9 August 1983.

27. Gill, *Gathered for Life,* p. 161.

28. The Rt. Rev. Bishop Arne Rudvin, interview with the author, Karachi, 30 November 1983.

29. Philip Potter, press conference at Vancouver Assembly, Vancouver, 10 August 1983, author's record.

30. Emilio Castro, *General Secretary's Report to the Central Committee of the World Council of Churches,* Hannover, 11 August 1988: Document no. 47, p. 10.

Central American Liberation Theology: pp. 51-64

1. Juan Hernandez Pico, "The Experiment of Nicaragua's Revolutionary Christians," in *The Challenge of Basic Christian Communities,* ed. John Eagleson and Sergio Torres (New York: Orbis Books/Maryknoll, 1982), p. 69. On Christian participation in the Nicaraguan revolution, see Gerhard Koberstein, ed., *Nicaragua: Revolution und Christlicher Glaube* (Frankfurt: Verlag Otto Lempeck, 1982).

2. Philip Berryman, "The Religious Roots of Rebellion," in *Christians in the Central American Revolutions* (London: SCM Press, 1984), p. 51.

3. Gustavo Gutierrez, *A Theology of Liberation: History, Politics, and Salvation* (London: SCM Press, 1975), p. 202.

4. Ibid., p. 272.

5. *Ecumenical Press Service,* 21 August 1979.

6. On Freire and his ecumenical background, see Jean G.H. Hoffmann, "Genfer 'Erziehung zur Befreiung.' Das Revolutionaere Bildungsprogramm des Paulo Freire," in *Reich Gottes oder Weltgemeinschaft?,* ed. Beyerhaus and Kuenneth, p. 131.

7. Shirley Christian, *Nicaragua: Revolution in the Family* (New York: Random House, 1985), p. 281.

8. *Ecumenical Press Service,* 1-5 April 1983; *One World* (May 1983) pp. 4, 5.

9. Commision Nicaraguense de Juristas, *Informe 2 Cantidad de Prisioneros Asesinados por el FSLN.* Mimeo. (Undated)

10. Christian, *Nicaragua,* p. 281.

11. Gill, *Gathered for Life,* pp. 159, 160.

12. Quoted in the *Congressional Record,* Senate, 14 February 1983, p. S1131.

13. *Informationsdienst Glaube in der zweiten Welt* no. 15 (25 August 1982): p. 5.

14. *Ecumenical Press Service,* 25 September 1981.

15. *International Herald Tribune,* 11 July 1984.

16. *Nicaragua: The Human Rights Record* (London: Amnesty International, March 1986), p. 21.

17. Dr. Emilio Castro, interview with author, Geneva, 12 July 1984.

18. Bernard Nietschmann, statement before the Organization of American States' Commission on Human Rights, 3 October 1983, p. 5. Mimeo.

19. Bernard Nietschmann in letter dated 28 November 1983.

20. Ibid.

21. Gill, *Gathered for Life,* p. 159.

22. Malle Niilus, ed., *Miskitos. Nicaragua* (Geneva: World Council of Churches, 1984).

23. "Land Rights for Indigenous People," in *Program to Combat Racism (PCR) Information* (Geneva: World Council of Churches, 1983), no. 16.

24. Ibid., p. 8.

25. *Ecumenical Press Service*, 28 February-6 March 1982.

26. J.A. Emerson Vermaat,*Wall Street Journal* (European edition), 4 April 1984.

27. Gill, *Gathered for Life*, p. 160

28. *One World* (October/November 1983): p. 5.

29. Ibid.

30. *Ecumenical Press Service*, 26-30 September 1983.

31. Ibid.

32. *Ecumenical Review* vol. 36: no. 1 (1984): pp. 108, 109.

33. World Council of Churches Central Committee press conference, Buenos Aires, 30 July 1985, author's record.

34. Ibid.

35. Ibid. At the conference, the author asked members of the World Council of Churches' delegation if they had seen representatives of the Permanent Commission on Human Rights or the Roman Catholic hierarchy in Nicaragua. The answer was "No."

36. "Pastoral Letter to the People of the Churches of Central America," *Ecumenical Review* no. 4 (October 1985): p. 500.

37. See *Peace Courier* (April 1984): p. 8.

38. *Neues Deutschland*, 10-11 August 1985, p. 1.

39. Text provided by the United States Information Agency, United States Embassy, The Hague, 1 March 1982.

40. Gill, *Gathered for Life*, p. 157.

41. Ibid., pp. 157, 158.

42. Ibid., p. 160.

43. Advertisement in *The Times*, 14 March 1980.

44. Ninan Koshy, interview with author, Geneva, 9 July 1984.

45. World Council of Churches, *Reports of the Churches in International Affairs, 1979-1982*, p. 127; Document no. 33 (Revised) World Council of Churches Central Committee, Geneva, 1980, p. 6.

46. Gill, *Gathered for Life*, p. 158. ·

47. World Council of Churches, *Your Kingdom Come*, p. 243.

48. Full text in *Ecumenical Press Service*, 1-10 January 1983.

49. World Council of Churches, *Reports of the Churches in International Affairs, 1979-1982*, p. 125.

50. Gill, *Gathered for Life*, p. 160.

51. *Ecumenical Press Service*, 2 October 1981.

52. Alexander Haig, *Caveat: Realism, Reagan, and Foreign Policy* (London: Weidenfeld and Nicolson, 1984), p. 103.

53. U.S. Department of State, "El Salvador: The Search for Peace," in *Department of State Bulletin*, October 1981, p. 74.

54. U.S. Department of State and U.S. Department of Defense, *Background Paper: Central America*, 27 May 1983, p. 6.

55. Author's interviews with two former Nicaraguan customs officials, San José (Costa Rica), 25, 27 August 1986.

56. *The Economist's Foreign Report*, 4 June 1981.

57. Roy Godson, ed., *Intelligence Requirements for the 1980s: Intelligence and Policy* (Lexington: Lexington Books, 1986), pp. 157, 158.

58. World Council of Churches, *Reports of the Churches in International Affairs, 1970-1973*, p. 211.

59. See also *Ecumenical Press Service*, 24 March 1977.

60. *One World* (May 1980): p. 21.

Southern Africa and the WCC's Program to Combat Racism: pp. 65-76

1. World Council of Churches, *Report of the World Consultation on Racism on Churches Responding to Racism in the 1980s* (Geneva: World Council of Churches, 1983), p. 80.

2. World Council of Churches press conference at Noordwijkerhout, 19 June 1980, author's record.

3. Ibid.

4. Document no. 17, World Council of Churches Central Committee, Jamaica, 1979, p. 2. Also Minutes and Reports of World Council of Churches Central Committee Meeting, Nottingham, 1969, p. 272.

5. *Der Spiegel*, 31 July 1978, p. 85.

6. "Soviet, East German, and Cuban Involvement in Fomenting Terrorism in Southern Africa," in U.S. Congress, Senate, Committee of the Judiciary, *Report of the Chairman of the Subcommittee on Security and Terrorism*, 97th Cong., 2nd sess.. 1982, p. 14.

7. *Algemeen Dagblad*, 8 November 1978.

8. *Trouw*, August 1978.

9. *Ecumenical Press Service*, 10 February 1977.

10. *Newsweek* (International Edition), 3 July 1978, p. 15; *Elseviers Magazine*, 1 July 1978, p. 45; *Algemeen Dagblad*, 26 June 1978.

11. Document no. 4, World Council of Churches Executive Committee, Helsinki, September 1978, p. 4; *One World* (July-August 1977).

12. *Nederlands Dagblad*, 13 September 1978.

13. Ibid.

14. *Newsweek* (International Edition), 18 September 1978, p. 23.

15. *Ecumenical Press Service*, 14 September 1978.

16. World Council of Churches press briefing, Ecumenical Center, Geneva, 2 November 1978, author's record. A report of Nkomo's remarks was published in *Newsweek* (International Edition), 18 September 1978, p. 24.

17. World Council of Churches Central Committee meeting, Kingston, Jamaica, 1 January 1979, author's record.

18. *Ecumenical Press Service*, 12 October 1978.

19. Ibid., 26 October 1978.

20. World Council of Churches Central Committee meeting, Kingston, Jamaica, 10 January 1979, author's record.

21. *Ecumenical Review* vol. 31: no. 2 (April 1979): p. 201.

22. Document No. 44A, World Council of Churches Central Committee, Jamaica, 1979, pp. 1, 2.

23. *Ecumenical Press Service,* 3 September 1981.

24. Archbishop Edward Scott and Philip Potter, "Letter to Salvation Army," *Ecumenical Press Service,* 3 September 1981.

25. Gill, *Gathered for Life,* pp. 151, 152.

26. Ibid., p. 153.

27. *Ecumenical Press Service,* 20 September 1979.

28. Ibid., 27 March 1980.

29. John Kurewa, "Zimbabwe is Born" in *Ecumenical Press Service,* 1 May 1980.

30. Document No. 23, World Council of Churches Central Committee, Geneva, 1980, p. 10.

31. *The Times,* 10 September 1980.

32. *The Sunday Times,* 27 March 1983.

33. *Ecumenical Press Service,* 28 February-6 March 1982.

34. *One World,* July/August 1983, p. 5.

35. *Newsweek* (International Edition), 7 May 1984, p. 21.

36. *Ecumenical Press Service,* 21-30 November 1983.

37. Ninan Koshy, in response to question posed by author at a World Council of Churches press conference, Geneva, 11 July 1984, author's records.

38. Gill, *Gathered for Life,* p. 154.

39. *Ecumenical Press Service,* 4 December 1985.

40. Document no. 17, World Council of Churches Central Committee, Jamaica, 1979, p. 17.

41. *Ecumenical Press Service,* 6 December 1985.

42. *Reformatorisch Dagblad,* 10 December 1985; *Nederlands Dagblad,* 11 December 1985.

43. World Council of Churches, *A Challenge to the Church. A Theological Comment on the Political Crisis in South Africa. The Kairos Document and Commentaries* (Geneva: PCR Information, Special Issue, November 1985), pp. 18, 30.

At Odds in the Middle East: pp. 77-84

1. Gill, *Gathered for Life,* pp. 148, 149.

2. Ibid., p. 149.

3. World Council of Churches, *Reports of the Churches in International Affairs, 1970-1973,* p. 215.

4. Ibid., p. 218.

5. Ibid., p. 215.

6. Paton, *Breaking Barriers,* p. 163.

7. Yassir Arafat, "Message to the World Council of Churches' General Assembly Meeting in Nairobi," Beirut, Lebanon, 14 November 1975, pp. 1, 2. Mimeo.

8. *Ecumenical Press Service,* 6-10 December 1982.

9. World Council of Churches Central Committee press release through *Ecumenical Press Service,* Geneva, July 1984.

10. *Ecumenical Press Service,* 6-10 December 1982.

11. Gill, *Gathered for Life,* p. 148.

12. World Council of Churches, *Reports of the Churches in International Affairs 1974-1978,* pp. 198, 199.

13. World Council of Churches, "World Council of Churches Team's Visit to Iraq," in Commission of the Churches on International Affairs, *CCIA Newsletter* no. 5 (1975): pp. 12, 13.

14. World Council of Churches, "Human Rights in the West Bank," *CCIA Background Information* no. 1 (1983): p. 5.

15. Betz and Beyerhaus,*Oekumene im Spiegel von Nairobi,* pp. 252, 253.

16. Rabbi A. J. Wolf, "Als Rabbi in Nairobi," in *Oekumenische Rundschau* no. 2 (1976): p. 309.

17. Minutes of World Council of Churches Central Committee Meeting, West Berlin, 1974, p. 39.

18. Minutes of World Council of Churches Central Committee Meeting, Geneva, 1980, p. 67.

19. *Ecumenical Press Service,* 18 September 1980.

20. Minutes of World Council of Churches Central Committee Meeting, Jamaica, 1979, pp. 72, 73.

21. World Council of Churches Central Committee meeting, Jamaica, 9 January 1979, author's record.

22. *Ecumenical Press Service,* 21 May 1981.

23. "Invasion of Lebanon" in *CCIA Background Information,* no. 2 (1982): p. 5.

24. Minutes of World Council of Churches Central Committee Meeting, Geneva, 1982, pp. 84, 85.

25. Ibid., p. 85.

26. Ibid., p. 82.

27. Ibid.

28. Mario Miegge, "Reflections on Terrorism in Italy," in *CCIA Background Information* no. 5 (1978): p. 14.

29. World Council of Churches, *Reports of the Churches in International Affairs, 1979-1982,* p. 144.

30. *Ecumenical Press Service,* 26-30 April 1980.

31. *New York Times,* 30 April 1986.

Nuclear Disarmament: Tilting Toward the Soviet Line: pp. 85-94

1. World Council of Churches, *Target,* daily newspaper of the Nairobi Assembly, 22 November 1975, p. 3.

2. World Council of Churches Central Committee meeting, Jamaica, 2 January 1979, author's record.

3. Miklos, "Some Experience of the Policy Regarding Churches," pp. 10, 11.

4. Paton, *Breaking Barriers,* p. 140.

5. Ibid., p. 182.

6. World Council of Churches "Report of the Consultation on Militarism," in *CCIA Background Information* no. 2 (1978): p. 4.

7. See also Paulos Gregorios, "Is There No Balm in Gilead?" in Document no. PD 25, Fifth Assembly of the World Council of Churches, Nairobi, 1975.

8. World Council of Churches, "Report of the Consultation on Militarism," p. 10.

9. Ibid., p. 8.

10. *Ecumenical Press Service,* 20 April 1978.

11. Documents of the World Council of Churches and the Roman Catholic church, "Peace and Disarmament" (Geneva: World Council of Churches and Rome: Pontifical Commission Iustitia et Pax, 1982), pp. 87, 88.

12. World Council of Churches, *CCIA Background Information* no. 6 (1978): p. 14.

13. Ibid., p. 17.

14. Document no. 10, World Council of Churches Central Committee, Jamaica, 1979, p. 9.

15. Paul Abrecht, ed., *Faith and Science in an Unjust World: Report of the World Council of Churches' Conference on Faith, Science, and the Future* (Geneva: World Council of Churches, 1980), vol. 2, p. 170.

16. Ibid., p. 171.

17. Ibid., pp. 320, 323.

18. Roger L. Shinn, ed., *Faith and Science in an Unjust World,* vol. 1, p. 324.

19. Ibid., p. 325.

20. See North Atlantic Treaty Organization, *Facts and Figures* (Brussels: North Atlantic Treaty Organization Information Service, 1981), p. 294, for the text of a communique issued on 12 December 1979, following a special meeting of NATO foreign and defense ministers.

21. Ibid., p. 295.

22. *Ecumenical Press Service,* 21 February 1980.

23. "Arms Race in Europe: New Developments," in *CCIA Background Information* no. 3 (1980): p. 5.

24. Document no. 33 (Revised), World Council of Churches Central Committee, Geneva, 1980, p. 1.

25. Committee on Unit II, Justice and Service, Report of Subgroup 3, World Council of Churches Central Committee, Geneva 1980, p. 3.

26. World Council of Churcnes Central Committee meeting, Geneva, 22 August 1980, author's record.

27. *Neue Zeit,* 17 August 1981, p. 1.

28. World Council of Churches Central Committee meeting, Dresden, 17 August, 1981, author's record.

29. World Council of Churches, *Reports of the Churches in International Affairs, 1979-1982,* pp. 45, 46, 47.

30. Paul Abrecht and Ninan Koshy, eds., *Before It's Too Late: The Challenge of Nuclear Disarmament* (Geneva: World Council of Churches, 1983), p. 29.

31. Ibid., p. 32.

32. Ibid., pp. 8, 31.

33. William Sloane Coffin, Jr., "It's a Sin to Build a Nuclear Weapon," sermon delivered in Amsterdam, Holland, 22 November 1981, p. 3. Mimeo.

34. World Council of Churches, *Reports of the Churches in International Affairs, 1979-1982,* p. 55.

35. Document no. 25, World Council of Churches Central Committee, Geneva, 1982, pp. 3, 19.

36. Minutes of World Council of Churches Central Committee Meeting, Geneva, July 1982, p. 18.

37. Ibid., p. 76.

38. Dorothee Soelle, "Life in Its Fullness," in Document TH3-1, World Council of Churches Vancouver Assembly, 1983, pp. 6, 7.

39. Gill, *Gathered for Life,* p. 75.

40. Ibid., pp. 73, 74.

41. Ibid., pp. 75, 76.

42. Ibid., p. 134.

43. Ibid., p. 135.

New Directions for the WCC: pp. 95-103

1. Daniel Patrick Moynihan, *A Dangerous Place* (London: Secker and Warburg, 1979), p. 159.

2. Dean Vladimir Rusak in a letter to the World Council of Churches' Vancouver Assembly, 1983, obtained from Keston College, England.

3. Quoted in *NRC Handelsblad*, 9 August 1983.

4. Ibid.

5. Weingartner, "Human Rights on the Ecumenical Agenda," p. 24.

6. Quoted in Paul Hollander, *Political Pilgrims: Travels of Western Intellectuals to the Soviet Union, China, and Cuba* (New York: Harper Colophon, 1983), p. 70.

7. Bishop Sydney Charles and Archdeacon Hoskin Huggins, St. George's, Grenada, interviews with author, 30 March and 1 April 1984. For statements by the Grenada Council of Churches in support of the U.S. military action, see *One World* (March 1984): p. 4. For further documentation, see J.A. Emerson Vermaat, "Church and State In Grenada During the Bishop Regime, 1979-1983," in *Religion in Communist Lands* no. 2 (Spring 1986): pp. 53, 54.

8. *One World* (July/August 1983): p. 7.

9. Alvaro Oviedo, "Theology of Liberation: A New Heresy?" in *World Marxist Review* no. 3 (March 1986): p. 90.

10. *The Times*, 5 December 1985, p. 7.

11. Philip Potter, interview with author, Geneva, 22 August 1980.

12. Gill, *Gathered for Life*, p. 149.

13. Ibid., p. 162.

14. Helmut Thielicke, *Theological Ethics* (Grand Rapids: William B. Eerdmans, 1979), vol. 2: p. 499.

Index

Afghanistan, 96, 100-102
    refugees, 39
    Soviet invasion of, 39-50
    U.N. actions, 47-50
Africa, guerrilla war in, 67-69,
    73-74
African National Congress, 66-67
Afro-Asian People's Solidarity
    Organization, 7
aggression, WCC position on, 39-40
Ajamian, Archbishop, 82
Albania, 9
Amin, Hafizullah, 39
Amnesty International, 54
Angola, 12
apartheid, 65-66, 71, 76
Aquino, Corazon, 37
Arafat, Yasar, 78
Arbatov, Georgi, 91
arms race (See nuclear disarmament)
Armstrong, James, 48-49
Asia:
    human rights in, 27-37
    one-party states in, 30
    Soviet policy, 37
Assembly (WCC), 3-4

Bahr, Egon, 91
Banana, Canaan, 75
Begin, Menachem, 81
Bichkov, Alexey, 45
Blake, Eugene Carson, 9-11, 77-78
boat people, 29
Bourdeaux, Michael, 20-21
Brezhnev, Leonid, 91
Buddhists, in Vietnam, 29
Buehrig, Marga, 58
Buevski, Alexey, 14, 15, 85, 90

Cambodia, 27, 29
    mass killings in, 30-31, 44
    Vietnamese invasion, 31-32

Camp David Accords, 80-81
capitalism, WCC position on, 65-66,
    86-87
Castro, Emilio, 6, 49, 54
Catholic Church:
    "popular church" in Nicaragua,
    53-54
    relations with WCC, 3
    in Vietnam, 29
Central America, 51-64
    liberation theology in, 51-52
    U.S. policy in, 101
Central Committee (WCC), 3-4
Chandra, Romesh, 7
Chao, T. C., 40
Chiang Ching-Kuo, 35
China, People's Republic of:
    admission to U.N., 34-35
    human rights in, 34
China, Republic of (Taiwan), 34-35
Christianity:
    and Marxist revolution, 51-52
    moral tradition of, 102
Christian Peace Conference, 6,
    14-15, 19, 46, 58, 85, 91, 97
Church and Society in Latin
America
    (ISAL), 6
churches, WCC-member, 95-97
    political influences on, 95-96
Coffin, William Sloane, Jr., 84, 91
Commission of the Churches on
    International Affairs, 5-7
Commission on Inter-church Aid,
    Refugee, and World Service,
    32-33
Commission on the Churches'
    Participation in Development
    (CCPD), 64
Communism (See Marxism)
Communist front organizations, 6-7,
    96-97, 101

Conference for Caribbean Churches, 64
Conference of European Churches, 18-19
Cuba, 62-64
Cuban Resource Center, 64
Czechoslovakia, 40

de Lange, H. M., 86
De Santa Ana, Julio, 6
d'Escoto, Miguel, 58
Diaz, Silvio, 57

disarmament (See nuclear disarmament)
dissidents:
Chinese, 34
Soviet, 23, 97-99
Dobrynin, Anatoly, 62
Duarte, José Napoleon, 59
Dudko, Dimitri, 21

ecumenical movement, politicization of, 1
education, mass, 52
Education and Renewal program unit, 4
Egypt, 80-81
Elliot, Canon, 69
El Salvador, 42, 52, 58, 59-64, 99
Evangelic Council of Churches of Cuba, 64
Executive Committee (WCC), 3-4

Faith and Order movement, 2-3, 99
Faith and Witness program unit, 4
Filaret, Metropolitan, 22
Finney, Charles, 2
Freire, Paulo, 52
Fretelin, 67

General Secretary (WCC), 3-4
genocide, in Nicaragua, 54
German Evangelical Church, 69, 79
González, José Esteban, 52-53
Gorbachev, Mikhail, 24-25

Gregorios, Paulos Mar, 6, 30, 58, 91, 92
Grenada, 98
Gromyko, Andrei, 87
Guatemala, 58
guerrilla war:
in Africa, 67-69, 73-74
in El Salvador, 59-61, 63

Habgood, John, 94
Haig, Alexander, 62
Haiti, 33
Hansen, Paul, 18
Harper, Charles R., 53, 58
Headlam, A. C., 2-3
Hebly, J. A., 19
Helsinki Accords, 13-14, 16-17
Hernandez, Lino, 53
Holloway, Richard, 13, 15
Honduras, 58
Honecker, Erich, 90
Hsu, Victor W. C., 7
human rights:
in Soviet bloc, 12-25, 97-98
WCC position on, 12, 97-99
Human Rights Day, 35
Hungarian Reformed Church, 85
Hungary, 18

imperialism, WCC position on, 65
indigenous peoples (See minorities)
Indochina:
communist expansion in, 27-28
war in, 27-32
INF Treaty, 94
International Association of Democratic Lawyers, 68
International Jewish Committee for Interreligious Consultation, 80
International Missionary Council, 2, 3
Iran, 83
Iraq, 79
Ireland, 69
Israel, 77-82

Italian Communist Party, 82
Italy, 82

Jerusalem, 80
Jews:
Soviet, 66
WCC position on, 79
John Paul II, 53, 93
Justice and Service program unit, 4-5

Kairos Document, 75-76
Kampuchea (See Cambodia)
Kao, Reverend, 35
Kaohsiung incident, 35
Keston College, 20
Khmer Rouge, 31
Khomeini, Ayatollah, 83
Kirill, Archbishop, 40-41, 44-45, 48, 88
Korea (See North Korea; South Korea)
Korean War, 28, 39-40, 46
Koshy, Ninan, 6, 7, 11, 23, 46, 61, 78-79, 81
Kuo Min-Tang, 34-35
Kurds, 79

Langhoff, Johannes, 44
Laos, 27, 29
Latin America:
Soviet policy, 62-64
U.S. in, 55-64, 101
Lebanon, 81-82
leftism, in WCC, 11-12
liberation movements (See also revolution)
WCC support of, 66-76, 100-102
liberation theology, 3, 41-42, 51-52, 97
Marxism and, 99
WCC position on, 52, 59, 99-101
Libya, 83-84
Life and Work movement, 2-3
literacy campaigns, 52

Loenning, Per, 17, 44, 82
Luwuum, Archbishop, 98

Makary, Archbishop, 43
Malik, Alexander, 47-48
Maoism, 34
Marcos, Fernando, 36-37
Marxism:
and Christianity, 51-52
and liberation theology, 99
Matabeleland, 73-74
Matheson, Alan, 33
Melbourne conference (1980), 41-44
Middle East, 77-84
terrorism, 77-78, 82-84
Miklos, Imre, 85
militarism, WCC position on, 86-87
minorities, WCC position on, 54-57
Miskito Indians, 54-57
missionary movements, 1-2
Mitton, Stanley, 79
Montefiore, Hugh, 88
Montreux colloquium on the Helsinki Accords, 16-17
Moody, Dwight L., 2
Moravian Church, 55, 57
Moynihan, Daniel Patrick, 95
Mugabe, Robert, 67-68, 72-75
Muzorewa, Abel, 67, 74

Nairobi Assembly, 12-17, 30, 85, 86
National Council of Churches, 61
Nazir-Ali, Michael, 43
Nicaragua, 51-59, 61-64, 99-100
Nietschmann, Bernard, 55
Niilus, Leopoldo, 5-6, 36, 89
Nikodim, Metropolitan, 6, 13, 14, 21, 42
Nkomo, Joshua, 67-68, 72-73
Nolde, O. Frederick, 5
North Atlantic Treaty Organization, 87, 96
nuclear missile deployment, 40-41, 88-90
North Korea, 28, 35-36, 39-40
North Vietnam, 27-28

Norway, Church of, 69
Norwegian Missionary Society, 69
nuclear deterrence, WCC position
on, 90-94

nuclear disarmament:
Soviet proposals, 85-86
unilateral, 88
U.N. session on, 87
WCC position on, 85-94
nuclear missiles:
NATO deployment of, 40-41,
88-90
Soviet, 89
Nujoma, Sam, 66

Obando y Bravo, Miguel, 53, 54, 58
Ortega, Daniel, 58

Palestine Liberation Organization,
67, 77-79, 82-83, 100
Palme, Olof, 91
Paris Peace Agreement (Vietnam
War), 27-28
Pastora, Edén, 52
Patriotic Front (Zimbabwe), 67-75
Pena, Amana, 54
Pentecostals, Soviet, 20, 23
Permanent Commission on Human
Rights (CPDH, Nicaragua), 52, 58
persecution of religion (See
religious persecution)
Philippines, 23
human rights in, 36-37
Pimen, Patriarch, 15-16, 22
Polisario Front, 67
political prisoners:
in China, 34
in Nicaragua, 52-53
in Vietnam, 28-29
Potter, Philip, 1, 7, 13, 17, 19,
22, 29, 30-31, 32-33, 35, 36,
45-46, 47, 49, 62, 69-70, 72,
79, 87, 98, 100
practical Christianity, 2
Presbyterian Church of Ireland, 69

Presbyterian Church of Taiwan,
34-35
Presidents (WCC), 4
press censorship, 57
Preus, David, 48
Prins, Simon, 47
Program for Disarmament and
Against Militarism and the Arms
Race (PDAM), 85-94
Program to Combat Racism, 5,
65-66
äprogram units (WCC), 4-5

racism:
in Soviet Union, 66
WCC position on, 65-76
Raiser, Konrad, 21, 36
refugees:
Afghan, 39
Vietnamese, 32-33
Regelson, Lev, 9, 20-22
religious persecution:
in Nicaragua, 53-54
in Soviet bloc, 9-11, 13-25, 97-98
in Vietnam, 29
WCC position on, 29
revival movements, 2
revolution (See also liberation
movements)
Christianity and, 51-52
WCC position on, 99-101
Rhodesia (See Zimbabwe)
Rossel, Jacques, 13, 15
Rudvin, Arne, 49
Rusak, Vladimir, 22-23, 97
Russell, David, 69-70
Russian Orthodox church, 7, 13-16,
18-25, 40, 41, 42-43, 47, 85,
96-98
dissidents within, 97-98
persecution of, 9-11

Sadat, Anwar, 80-81
Salonga, Jovito, 36
Salvation Army, 69-71
Sandinista Revolution, 51-59

Scoon, Paul, 98
Scott, Edward W., 13-14, 22
Shinn, Roger, 88
Siberia, 29
Siberian Seven, 20
"silent diplomacy," 98-99
Simatupang, Tahi B., 14
Sjollema, Baldwin, 66, 68
Soares, Mario, 7, 59
Social Gospel movement, 2
Soelle, Dorothee, 92
Somoza Debayle, Anastasio, 51
South Africa, 65-67, 71, 75-76, 98, 99, 100
South African Communist Party, 67
äSouth Korea, 35-36
South Vietnam, 27-28
South-West African People's Organization, 66-67
Soviet bloc, influences on WCC, 9-25
Soviet Union:
    Asian policy, 37
    current reforms in, 24-25
    disarmament proposals, 85-86
    dissidents, 23, 97-99
    human rights in, 12-25, 97-98
    invasion of Afghanistan, 39-50
    Jews in, 66
    Latin American policy, 62-64
    nuclear capability of, 89
    religion in, control of, 22-23, 96, 97-98
    religious persecution in, 9-11, 13-25, 98
    South African policy, 66-67
    support of liberation theology, 99
    Third World policy, 14-15
Special Fund to Combat Racism, 5, 66, 69-70
Spurgeon, Charles H., 2
Staalsett, Gunnar, 42
Syria, 82, 83

Taiwan (See China, Republic of)
Tambo, Oliver, 67

terrorism, WCC position on, 69, 77-78, 82-84
Thielicke, Helmut, 102
Third World:
    influence on WCC, 97
    Soviet influences on, 14-15
    WCC position on, 65, 102
Thompson, William P., 14, 48, 58, 81
't Hooft, W. A. Visser, 7
"threats to peace" statement, 40-41, 44-46
Ting, K. H., 34
Toth, Karoly, 19, 46, 91, 92
Tutu, Desmond, 100

Uganda, 98
Union of Evangelical Christian Baptists (USSR), 11
Unit Committees (WCC), 4-5
United African National Congress, 67
United Nations:
    and Afghanistan, 47-50
    China admitted to, 34-35
    disarmament proposals, 87
    politics in, 95
    resolution on Zionism, 79
    WCC relations with, 5
United Presbyterian Church (U.S.), 79
United States:
    in Latin America, 59-64, 101
    Philippine bases, 36-37
    in Vietnam War, 27-28
    WCC attitude toward, 59-64, 83-84, 101

Vancouver Assembly, 18, 22-24, 47-50, 53, 55, 59, 71, 75, 77, 83, 92-94, 100
Vietnam:
    human rights in, 28-34
    refugees, 32-33
    religion in, 29
Vietnam War, 27-28, 44, 100

Villas, Marianella Gracia, 52
Vos, Anton, 42

Waldheim, Kurt, 32
Warsaw Pact, 88-89
Wei Jingsheng, 34
Weingartner, Erich, 97, 99
West, the, WCC bias against, 96, 101
West Bank, 79
Williams, Harry, 69-70
Women's International Democratic Federation, 7
Wood, Wilfred, 66
World Council of Churches:
    criticisms of, 69-71
    international activities, 5-7
    member churches of, 95-97
    organizational structure, 3-5, 101
    origins of, 1-3
    politicization of, 1, 11-12, 95-97, 101-102
    programs of, 4-5
    protest policies of, 98-99
    spiritual aims of, 102
    suggestions for improvement, 95-103
World Federation of Democratic Youth, 7
World Missionary Conference (1910), 2
World Peace Council, 6, 7, 46, 58, 59
World Student Christian Federation, 6

Yakunin, Gleb, 9, 20-22
Yakunin-Regelson letter, 9, 12-17, 19-22, 23, 99
Yuvenaliy, Metropolitan, 13, 21-22, 48

ZANU, 67-69
Zimbabwe, 67-75
Zionism, 79

FREEDOM HOUSE BOOKS

General Editor: James Finn

YEARBOOKS

Freedom in the World: Political Rights and Civil Liberties,
Raymond D. Gastil; annuals from 1978-1988.

STUDIES IN FREEDOM

Escape to Freedom: The Story of the International Rescue Committee,
Aaron Levenstein; 1983.
Forty Years: A Third World Soldier at the UN,
Carlos P. Romulo (with Beth Day Romulo); 1986. *(Romulo: A Third
World Soldier at the UN,* paperback edition, 1987.)
Today's American: How Free?
James Finn & Leonard R. Sussman, (Eds.); 1986.
Will of the People: Original Democracies in Non-Western Societies, Raul
S. Manglapus; 1987.

PERSPECTIVES ON FREEDOM

Three Years at the East-West Divide,
Max M. Kampelman; (Introductions by Ronald Reagan and Jimmy
Carter; edited by Leonard R. Sussman); 1983.
*The Democratic Mask: The Consolidation
of the Sandinista Revolution,*
Douglas W. Payne; 1985.
The Heresy of Words in Cuba: Freedom of Expression & Information,
Carlos Ripoll; 1985.
Human Rights & the New Realism: Strategic Thinking in a New Age,
Michael Novak; 1986.
To License A Journalist?,
Inter-American Court of Human Rights; 1986.
The Catholic Church in China, L. Ladany; 1987.
Glasnost: How Open? Soviet & Eastern European Dissidents; 1987.
Yugoslavia: The Failure of "Democratic" Communism; 1987.
The Prague Spring: A Mixed Legacy Jiri Pehe, ed. 1988.
Romania: A Case of "Dynastic" Communism. 1989.

FOCUS ON ISSUES

*Big Story: How the American Press and Television Reported and
Interpreted the Crisis of Tet-1968 in Vietnam and Washington,*
Peter Braestrup; Two volumes 1977;
One volume paperback abridged 1978, 1983.
Soviet POWs in Afghanistan,
Ludmilla Thorne; 1986.
Afghanistan: The Great Game Revisited,
edited by Rossane Klass; 1988.
Nicaragua's Continuing Struggle: In Search of Democracy,
Arturo J. Cruz; 1988.
La Prensa: The Republic of Paper,
Jaime Chamorro Cardenal; 1988.
The World Council of Churches & Politics, 1975-1986
J.A. Emerson Vermaat, 1989.

AN OCCASIONAL PAPER

General Editor: **R. Bruce McColm**

Glasnost and Social & Economic Rights
Valery Chalidze, Richard Schifter; 1988.